Praise for Judy Greer's

I Don't Know What
You Know Me From

"If you've heard Judy speak even once you can hear her voice all through these wonderful stories, because she writes like she talks and what she says is so much fun to listen to. My only complaint was how much I missed her when the book was over—but that's how I always feel after a long stay with a good friend."

—Jim Parsons, star of *The Big Bang Theory*

"The book is so funny it might make her a household name."

—*Ladies' Home Journal*

"She's nothing if not honest—sometimes brutally so."

—*Los Angeles Times*

"Her book is just as honest, witty, and observant as she actually is. From her early life and her experiences in love and friendship to the weird world of Hollywood, she candidly spills the beans and consistently entertains. So now is your chance—you too can be friends with Judy (sort of)."

—Rashida Jones

"Charming. . . . [Greer's] bubbly best-friend personality and self-deprecating anecdotes will have readers rooting for her."   —*Booklist*

"Greer is an engaging and witty storyteller, at turns wistful and unsparingly honest."   —*Kirkus Reviews*

"I read it in one sitting. Then I flushed."
                                                —Zach Galifianakis

JUDY GREER

I Don't Know What You Know Me From

Judy Greer was born in Detroit and studied at The Theatre School, DePaul University's prestigious theater conservatory program. She is one of the most prolific actresses of her time, appearing to date in more than eighty roles across film and television, most notably in the Oscar-winning film *The Descendants*. No stranger to the small screen, she stars in the sitcom *Married*, voices a character on the cult hit *Archer*, and can also be seen in *Arrested Development*. Greer recently made her Broadway debut in *Dead Accounts*. Online, she stars in her own Yahoo! series called *Reluctantly Healthy*. Greer currently lives in Los Angeles.

I Don't Know What You Know Me From

My Life as a Co-Star

JUDY GREER

ANCHOR BOOKS

A DIVISION OF PENGUIN RANDOM HOUSE LLC · NEW YORK

For Dean Johnsen, who is everything.

FIRST ANCHOR BOOKS EDITION, APRIL 2015

Copyright © 2014, 2015 by Judy Greer

All rights reserved. Published in the United States by Anchor Books, a division of Penguin Random House LLC, New York, and distributed in Canada by Random House of Canada, a division of Penguin Random House Ltd., Toronto. Originally published in hardcover by Doubleday, a division of Penguin Random House LLC, New York, in 2014.

The Library of Congress has catalogued the Doubleday edition as follows:
Greer, Judy, 1975–
I don't know what you know me from : confessions of a co-star / Judy Greer. — First edition.
pages cm
1. Greer, Judy, 1975– 2. Actors—United States—Biography. I. Title.
PN2287.G6855A3 2014   791.4502'8092—dc23   [B]   2013036038

Anchor Books Trade Paperback ISBN: 978-0-345-80673-4
eBook ISBN: 978-0-385-53789-6

www.anchorbooks.com

Printed in the United States of America
10 9 8 7 6 5 4 3 2

Contents

Part 2—Hollywood Life

Part 3—Real Life

I Don't Know What You Know Me From

Introduction

Dear Reader,

I am not a movie star. Chances are when you walked by my book and saw my face, you didn't know what my name was, but you knew that I looked familiar. Perhaps you think we have a friend in common—we don't. Or that I was in your sorority—I wasn't. Maybe you do know that I'm an actress, but you just don't know my name. You might remember me from as far back as The Wedding Planner *or as recent as* Arrested Development *or* Carrie. *It's hard to say, since I've had so many different jobs and played so many different characters. What are you into? What do you like to watch? Are you into movies or television? Indie films or blockbusters? See, if I had the time, and we were in the same room, I could sit down with you and maybe tell you what you liked me from. I would look at your age, sex, and clothing and probably be able to pinpoint what role I've played that you responded to. It's a little like racial profiling, but with fans: fan profiling. (I'm sorry for mentioning racial profiling so early; it's probably made you uncomfortable, and that wasn't my intention.) Anyway, I don't know what you know me from, and it's taken fifteen years but I'm pretty good at fan profiling now. And I'd like to take this opportunity to thank you for being a fan, thank you for watching whatever it was that you watched, liking me, and buying my book. Unless we really do know each other, in which case, well, I'm sorry I didn't remember, and I'd still like to thank you for buying my book.*

I'm a nice girl from the Detroit area—Livonia, to be exact. I was born in Detroit, lived in Redford until my first memory, which my mom claims is of the linoleum kitchen floor in our first house. I went to high school in Livonia. (Go, Chargers! I never went to a single football game.) Then I went off to college in Chicago to study acting and never came back. OK, I'm exaggerating; I came back for my Christmas presents every year, which made me a deserving victim of the "we turned your bedroom into a den" cliché. I took a trip to Los Angeles after college, and fifteen years later I'm still here. It was February, can you blame me? Have you experienced a negative-eighty-degree windchill before?

You've heard the phrase "There are no small roles, just small actors"? Well, I kind of disagree. There are small roles, but when you get a lot of them in a row, you can become a pretty successful actress, and that's what I've done. At least for now, I'm not saying I don't want bigger roles. I'm not that self-satisfied. And who knows how much longer I'll keep getting jobs. I don't have a crystal ball, and even if I did, I'd probably drop it by accident.

So this is me, just trying, in book form, to introduce myself. This is who I am. This is what I think about things. This is stuff that happened to me, that could just as easily have happened to you. I'm not that special, and we're prob-

ably not that different (unless you're a dude). I think I am really lucky to be where I am in life, but I've never really lost the feeling that I don't fit in, and if you have, will you please e-mail me and tell me how you did it? I'm serious. Oh, and spoiler alert, I don't list all my credits in this book, so reading it will not tell you what you know me from—you'll have to Google me to figure that out. And hopefully, after reading this, you'll want to.

Love,
Judy Greer

Part 1

Early Life

Detroit-ish

I GREW UP IN A SUBURB OF DETROIT, MICHIGAN. NO, not Grosse Pointe. Not 8 Mile. To everyone who is not from Michigan: there are more places besides Grosse Pointe and 8 Mile in the Detroit area. Grosse Pointe is for superrich people, of which I was/am not. And 8 Mile is a road, not a place. It is a long road that goes from Eminem-land all the way to McMansion-land. I am from Livonia. It's basic. It's clean and there are no tall buildings that I can remember, maybe the city hall, or the hospital, but I'm only talking eight floors, tops. There are a lot of strip malls and two-story colonial houses and many good public schools. It is your typical midwestern suburb.

In Livonia our high schools were named after foreign statesmen, the junior highs were named after poets, and the elementary schools were named after presidents. I went to Kennedy for elementary school, Frost for middle, and Churchill for high school. But I hated school. I pretty much hated every second I had to be there. I can't really remember why I hated it so much, but I think some of it had to do with having to leave my house in the cold so many months out of the year. It was always so cold, and there was *a lot* of snow. I took the bus to high school, but most of elementary and all of junior high I had to walk. It was a particularly long walk across a huge field to get to Frost, and in the winter that field was covered in snow. There were no trees or buildings to stop the freezing-cold wind from tearing through my jacket and sweaters in order to get to the very center of my bones, where it would stay until spring. No, it wasn't uphill both ways barefoot, but still, those mornings and afternoons were rough. Sometimes my friend Nicole and I would "borrow" change from our classmates and stop at the donut shop on our walk home, and we'd cross the field almost happily, thinking of the cinnamon roll and hot chocolate we were about to inhale. And for one week during the summer I forgave that field because it would morph into a magical carny wonderland called the Livonia Spree. For one week I lived a block away from the Tilt-a-Whirl, the merry-go-round, the Matterhorn, game tents, a fun house, a house of horrors, and my favorite attraction, the Budweiser Clydesdale horses. I really looked forward to those horses coming to my town for a visit. I think that's why I cried so hard during that Super Bowl XLVII commercial. You know, the one about the horse trainer who sent his horse away to Budweiser once it was trained but then drove out to visit it during a nearby parade. And in the end the horse broke loose and ran back to find his trainer? Shit. Now I'm crying again. I sobbed after seeing that commercial. Like, *sobbed*. My husband was worried about me. I was worried about me; I wondered if people ever died of suffocation due to uncontrolled sobbing, because I thought I might. Anyway, as a kid I loved seeing those beer horses and marveled at their size. I always wondered if they liked being on the local carnival circuit and was slightly disillusioned when I found out there was more than one team of Budweiser Clydesdales. For years I thought I was meeting the stars of all those commercials. The day I found out differently was a real coming-of-age moment for me. Maybe *that's* why I cried so hard . . .

Before I ever went to Kennedy Elementary, I went to Gibson School for the Gifted, a private school for "gifted" students, as named. I like that they didn't mess around when naming it. So many private schools beat around the bush with names like Dalton and Spence, why not just say what it is? Crosley School for Rich Kids, or the Teeter School for Troublemakers, Lionsfront Last Chance Before Juvie Academy. Aren't we all thinking it anyway? At my gifted school for gifted students, we went to school until about 6:00 p.m., when they started to lock the doors and call the parents who hadn't picked their kids up yet (maybe they should have named it Gibson School for Children with Busy Parents). It was an ethnically diverse school; most of the students had divorced parents or came from households where both parents worked (me). I remember that my friend Chris and I were always the last ones to get picked up. I hated leaving Chris when my mom got there first because his parents were divorced and he could never remember which one was supposed to show up, but I hated it more when I was the last one, mostly because I was eight years old and eight-year-olds aren't usually that self-sacrificing. Chris could also be a little bit naughty. One day he wanted to start a gang, but since I was the only one left hanging around with him at the end of every day, it was just the two of us. He named us the Punk Rock Pick Lockers, and we managed, one time only, to pick a lock in the cafeteria and steal a mini carton of chocolate milk out of the refrigerator. I felt pretty cool after we picked our first lock but also completely scared we would get caught. And even though it was fun that day, I was certain that eventually Chris was going to get me in a lot of trouble. I couldn't be in a gang with this boy, that was not a "gifted" thing to do. I tried a phaseout, but it was hard since we were still the last two kids to get picked up after school every day. Shortly after our one and only gang activity, Chris came to school with a homemade puzzle and tried to give it to me. I refused, trying to make my motives clear. We could still hang out in the bookbinding corner after class, but accepting handmade gifts was where I drew the line. I could tell I hurt his feelings when I marched away from him, but I didn't care. I needed boundaries if I wasn't going to pursue a life of crime with him. That night when his dad finally came to pick Chris up, his dad found me and gave me the puzzle himself, telling me that Chris spent a lot of time making that puzzle for me and I should keep it. I put it together when they left and it said "I love you" on it. I felt terrible. I didn't know Chris *loved* me. I thought we were just friends and fellow gang members. *Now what do I do?* I thought. *Do I have to love him back? Or make him a puzzle that says, "OK . . ."?* When my parents pulled me out of Gibson after third grade, I didn't talk to Chris again until he magically showed up late in high school dating a tiny dancer I knew from the arts program. I was so happy to see his face, and happier to see that he didn't end up in jail, but we never really picked up where we left off and lost touch for good when I moved to Chicago.

I didn't want to change schools when I was at Gibson—that was my parents' idea. Even though my new school was just a short walk from our house, I did *not* want to go. I had friends at Gibson, they were all different colors, and probably brilliant and gifted and talented, but I didn't care about that stuff—they were my friends, and I didn't want to leave them. Everyone at public school seemed so average and white to me. My parents promised if I hated it, I could go back to Gibson, but they lied. Now that I'm an adult, I can't really blame them—it was expensive and a long drive—but still, for the record, they lied.

Once I left my special school, I never liked school again. It was all so normal. There were desks in rows, lesson plans, bells, after-school clubs that you had to be *invited* into. What's that all about? See, at Gibson we were told we were all amazing artists, that we were smart, creative, good writers, basically that we were special, but that we were equally special. I'm not saying this is how it should be, but it was hard to suddenly find out, at nine years old, that I didn't necessarily have all the talents I thought I did. For example, at my public school, there was an art club, and I didn't get invited to be in it. That was so confusing to me. Why couldn't anyone be in it if they wanted to, not just if the horse you drew actually looked like a horse? And how come in class we sat in desks instead of on couches or giant pillows? Why weren't there pets in every room? Why did I have to raise my hand to ask to go to the bathroom? Why didn't we call our teachers by their first names? It was a hard transition for me. I was graded for the first time in my life. I wasn't athletic, and I had weird hair, a combination that I blame for being a loner for a while. Is there some connection between "gifted" kids and weird hair? My old friends and I all had some crazy-ass hair, but at my public school everyone seemed to have great hair.

I thought since I was at a special school for special kids, public school would be a breeze for me, but it wasn't at first. (Of course I shouldn't rule out the possibility that I was in a school for weird or slow kids, but was lied to by my parents.) Eventually, I settled in and made friends, and even had some teachers who really inspired me. I resigned myself to not being popular but finding that one special friend who would always have my back. Her name was Nicole. She was pretty and smart and had great hair, of course. She was funny and just weird enough that she understood me and didn't think I was a spaz. She was also a great artist, so I always partnered with her to work on class projects (she totally got invited to be in art club, so we couldn't walk home together on Wednesdays after school). I was thrilled that we would go to the same junior high together so I didn't have to start from scratch again and find new friends. Nicole and I walked through that freezing-cold field together, side by side, and she stayed my best friend all through high school. This time we commuted by bus, unless one of us could con our parents into driving us instead.

I think that Nicole could have totally left me behind in junior high and been one of the popular girls, but she didn't. She looked like Grace Kelly when we were thirteen, and the boys really noticed her. I remember a boy asking me for my number, only to then call and ask for Nicole's. She went to homecoming with him, and I was 70/30 happy/jealous. I know I should have been 100 percent happy, but I was a teenage girl, for Christ's sake! And I am the John Hughes generation. I was waiting for my Blane, my Jake Ryan, and I am not a saint, I'm sorry, but I was a little jealous when Nicole got to go to a dance while I stayed home, wrote in my diary, and watched my VHS tape of *Pretty in Pink* again. In fact, the only high school dance I ended up going to was prom. I had my first boyfriend at that point, and Nicole had hers. We went together, naturally, and had a ball, kind of. My dad borrowed a fancy car for us to drive, and we got clearance to all spend the night at Nicole's date John's house because he had a cool apartment-style bedroom. I don't know how that became a winning argument with my parents, but they caved and that was the plan. I will just tell you right now I don't have a good prom story. It's hazy at best. And not hazy due to alcohol consumed that night, but probably more likely due to alcohol consumed since. I bought eight prom dresses, but none of them were right, so I ended up making my own out of a pattern from the 1960s I bought at a thrift store (hello, *Pretty in Pink* much?) and used my dress budget on fabulous shoes. Nicole bought her dress at a vintage store, and I thought we looked so cool I made my parents take our prom pictures in black and white to really capture our vintage vibe. Prom was in a fancy restaurant/venue in Dearborn (where the Big Three car companies used to live). I have to admit it was a little bit of a letdown after watching all those John Hughes movies leading up to it. Yes, it was beautifully decorated, and we all looked appropriately dressed up, but when I stepped into the room, there was no hush in the crowd, no one was shocked at my prom makeover, I didn't look better than the popular bitchy girls, none of them gave me a hesitant encouraging smile, there wasn't anyone apologizing for misjudging me the last four years, and worst of all Jake Ryan and Blane were nowhere to be found. But most shocking was I didn't care. We sat down for a few minutes, we danced for a few songs, then John went missing, and when we found him inhaling helium out of the decorative balloons in the corner, we decided to take off. We went to prom. Milestone checked off the list. We drove back to John's house, changed into our jeans and T-shirts, and watched *Sixteen Candles* until we fell asleep.

The best thing to me about growing up in a suburb of Detroit was going into Detroit—there was always great stuff to do there when I was a kid, and I actually did it. I am so happy, looking back, that my parents didn't hide out in their little suburb, that they took advantage of all the Motor City had to offer. There was a zoo, an awesome art museum with the most beautiful Diego Rivera mural you'll ever see, this gorgeous painting of an assembly line that is such a perfect representation of what Detroit was built on. A science center. The Red Wings played downtown, as did the Tigers. While I was in high school, they were renovating some old theaters in the city, and my first date with my first boyfriend, Eric Campbell, was to see *Casablanca* downtown at the Fox Theatre. It was the first time I'd ever seen the movie, and it was especially thrilling to see it on a big screen in a theater that it most likely played in the first time around. When I was little, there were lots of picnics, boat races, and Belle Isle, a little island/giant park that was connected to downtown by a bridge. But when I was old enough to go downtown with just my friends, I really fell in love with Detroit's music scene. There were great little bars and venues that local and touring bands would play in, and I tried to catch them all. I had a fake ID and I used it! There were great record stores, and with Ann Arbor about twenty minutes away in the opposite direction we Detroiters had great music at our fingertips.

I feel so brokenhearted today about the state of my hometown. As I write this, it's all over the news that Detroit has just filed for bankruptcy. My hometown is waving the white flag and admitting defeat. Maybe it's just because I'm from there, but I think there is something special about Detroit. It's like Detroit is America's sad family member who can't catch a break, a cautionary fable to teach our country a lesson—I just don't understand what the lesson is. Don't steal? Don't give up? Don't burn your shit down the night before Halloween? In my fantasy that city is like the Little Engine That Could. For so many years it was saying, "I think I can, I think I can, I think I can." Except in the Detroit version of that story, before getting to the top of the mountain, it stopped and said, "I can't." I want my little engine to get back to "I think I can." And eventually to "I *know* I can!" Detroit was a town of blue-collar workers. It created a middle class and, at one time, good-paying jobs with benefits for anyone, no matter one's education or color. It has an art museum, a symphony, it is the home of Motown, KISS, Jack White, and a cute zoo with all the main animals. And it made cars! Who loves their cars more than Americans? It has Lions and Tigers and Red Wings and Pistons. There's water everywhere and another country just a bridge or tunnel away. I am so lucky to be from Detroit, and I want so badly for it to get better, and now I feel terrible for abandoning it, but I have a lot of hope for my first home. It always took such good care of me, and I think it's time I pay a little back, or forward. There's still a lot of Detroit left in me, and even though I live in L.A. now, I'll always be a Punk Rock Pick Locker at heart.

I Used to Be More Ugly

I HATE WHEN I TELL PEOPLE I WAS UGLY AND THEY are like, "No . . . you're exaggerating." I really was; I have proof (see Ugly Judy 1). It's OK, I'm over it now, but I had an *extremely* long awkward phase that I think I am still (and might always be) recovering from. If I'm being honest, I believe that this is why I think I'm more attractive than I probably am. You see, when you are used to looking at this (see Ugly Judy 2) in the mirror every day for years, when you start to see this (see Pretty Judy), it looks pretty good, you know? I mean, trust me, I know I'm no Angelina Jolie (or insert person you think unreasonably beautiful here), but at least I don't look like my grandpa. (Sorry, Grandpa, I mean, you still landed my grandma, and she was smokin' so . . .)

When I was a kid, my mom didn't read me stories at night; she played these tapes of nursery rhymes for me that came with corresponding books. During the story a bell would sound for when you'd turn the page of the book. I got so good at following the bells that I took a book to preschool one day, gathered the other children around me in a circle, and read them my story. I had memorized the whole thing, including when to turn the page. When the teacher overheard me reading a book to the other kids,

TOP LEFT: Ugly Judy 1

TOP RIGHT: Ugly Judy 2

RIGHT: Pretty Judy

BOTTOM LEFT: Ugly Grandpa

BOTTOM RIGHT: Smokin' Hot
Grandma

she freaked out, called my mom at work, and told her that I was a genius and I could read. I was three. My mother asked what, exactly, I was reading, and when the teacher told her, my mom said, "She's not reading that book; she has it memorized. Is there anything else? I am in a meeting." My mom didn't suffer fools gladly.

My favorite book/tape my mom played for me was *The Ugly Duckling*. I felt, even at that young age, that the story of the ugly duckling was about me. I loved how the ugly duckling turned into a beautiful swan, and the older I got, and the uglier I got, the more I prayed that I would be like that duckling. This was the dawn of my ongoing obsession with makeover movies and makeovers in general. Don't all teenage girls have this phase? Even if it lands them in a Hot Topic or with a horrible perm? In retrospect, I feel like that story is full of shit, because, like, when have you ever seen an ugly duckling? They are the cutest little creatures out there. Not a one of them is even a little bit hard to swallow, visually speaking. But whatever, I didn't think of that when I was younger. I just wanted to believe that my transformation day would come. And it kind of did.

The summer between junior and senior years of high school was a big one for me. My hair magically grew overnight, I got my braces off, I started wearing contacts instead of glasses, and I got a real boyfriend!! Eric Campbell. He was cute, nice, funny, a whole year older than me, and about to start his first year of college at University of Michigan! *What?* That's not even the best part! He was also a drummer in an actual band that played rock concerts at bars and clubs in Detroit! I got to be a band girl! It was so awesome that I didn't even care that dating a drummer meant I always had to be there early to watch him set up and I always had to wait approximately one year after the show was over for him to pack up his drums. I didn't care about anything except that he liked me and he didn't go to my high school, which meant that he had no idea what it was like for me there. After that summer when I outgrew my "'FroMama" phase (thank you, Jason Baranowski, for that delightful nickname), I felt like my life was a John Hughes movie and I was having a major Ally Sheedy circa *The Breakfast Club* moment. I got a makeover and a boyfriend, but I still realized who I was on the inside and what was *really* important. Kind of.

College turned out to be an even better platform for a make-over. Now I was in a completely new place with all new people, and I was ready for a complete reinvention. I bleached out my 'fro and worked hard to shed the Michigan me. My mom's advice to me before I left for school in Chicago was "Don't shit where you eat." So, I also planned on playing impossible to get at my new school, too (it always works to make you more desirable and mysterious, unless no one wants to get you, in which case it just keeps you from hooking up with guys who will talk behind your back, win-win). College was when I felt like I really came into my own, except for one small mishap my first year. After several minutes of debilitating abdominal pain, I thought my appendix had ruptured in voice and speech class, but it turned out it was really just bad gas. Now, I just want to say in my own defense it wasn't me who demanded an ambulance be called and that I go to the ER—it was my teacher. And it wasn't my fault that the voice and speech room was on the third floor and that the EMTs had to carry me down three flights of stairs and through the lobby of the building in a stretcher-chair to the ambulance. I'm really not that high maintenance, usually. I did walk home after they diagnosed me as "gassy" in the ER. But besides that episode, I felt like the life I created in Chicago was what I wished my high school experience would have been like. I have always been a late bloomer, but I was really happy there and really grew up in those four years. By the time it was all over and I was ready to move to L.A., I felt like I had nailed it, nothing could get me down.

There is a TV movie called *Who Is Julia?* that I saw years ago. It's about a beautiful woman who gets in a terrible car accident, her face smashed beyond repair, so, as per usual, she has a face transplant. They replace her face with the face of a plain-looking lady who dropped dead of brain death (this is a direct quote from IMDb.com. They describe what happened to this character as "faints and suffers brain death." I swear I am not making that up). She goes from being this gorgeous woman to being, well, Mare Winningham. Moving to L.A. to be an actress made me feel like the Mare Winningham character in *Who Is Julia?* I went from feeling like I looked one way to learning that I looked totally different. *Everyone* here is gorgeous! Remember, this was before Judd Apatow made nerdy/dork/stoners the new black. I looked around the waiting room at auditions and felt like I was back in high school again. The people were dressed better than me, they were calmer than me, they seemed to use better deodorant, and most of all they were pretty. Like fashion-magazine pretty. Way prettier than me. For a while I got to audition for the lead roles, but they kept going to Pretty McPrettyson, and I began to get called in to play Pretty's best friend/sister/assistant. I had to stop reading the descriptions for the characters I was going in for. The descriptions, or breakdowns, as we Hollywood folk like to call them, were something like "all ethnicities, all ages, all sizes." Even my character in *The Wedding Planner* was supposed to be an overweight, middle-aged British woman. But how could I be upset? I was getting paid to act in a movie. Only one time do I remember my feelings getting hurt when the feedback from a casting director was that I wasn't ugly *enough*. In my mind the casting director was saying, "Yes, she's ugly. The character breakdown did call for ugly, and she is that, but we need even *more* ugly. Do you have anyone who is even uglier than this . . . oh, what's her name . . . oh, right, Judy Greer, do you represent anyone uglier than Judy Greer?" That one left a mark. But then

I remembered *Who Is Julia?* and it was Mare Winningham who was the star of the movie, not the car accident lady with no face left over, and wouldn't you rather have a long awesome life (read: career) than be gorgeous but dead (read: living with my parents again?). So maybe I don't look like Megan Fox, but I do OK, and if I hire a team of people to clean me, dress me, fix my hair, and paint my face and body, I can look above average on a red carpet for thirty minutes, which is plenty of time for my picture to be taken before I toss the Spanx, wipe off my lipstick, get a martini in my hand, and start having real fun.

Mom

MY MOTHER IS AN UNCONVENTIONAL PARENT, THANK God. She tried to be a normal mom, she tried to do the normal things, like cook dinner and host my birthday parties, but it just wasn't her. She is really impulsive. For example, if there was a blizzard outside but she wanted to go to the movies, we would go. We'd slide all over the road in her red Mustang driving there, but we would go. If she was on a diet, so were my father and I, and there were *a lot* of diets. We suffered through her chewing each bite of food thirty times, serving everything on dessert plates to make your meals look bigger, the Crock-Pot years, the aerobics classes, breakfast for dinner, no dinner. My poor dad . . . at least I got to leave for college.

There was also a lot of purging of our stuff and furniture rearranging. My mom has always been an early riser, and it was not uncommon for me to wake up around 11:00 a.m. on a Saturday and find that the living room was now in the dining room and that we actually no longer had a dining room but we did have a brand-new office. My father and I would get used to the changes, but then she would eventually just change them again. Leaving town without my mom could be stressful. You might come home to a new floor plan, half your wardrobe donated, and, sometimes, even a new dog. My dad is the opposite; he doesn't love change and likes to hang on to his possessions until he's sure there's no need or use for them anymore. This is hard on my mom, and during their last move she admitted to me that she was burning some of my dad's old books, magazines, and papers because she knew he would never get around to sorting through them in time for the movers to come. Like any good daughter would, I immediately called my dad and told on her. I probably should have let them work out their own problems, but I can never keep myself from butting into any situation, like someone else I know and love and am writing about at this exact moment.

There was always a lot of change happening. I liked it. It was exciting. I always felt the same rush my mom did after a day reorganizing the basement or driving a carload of stuff to the Goodwill. A fresh start, a new beginning, and it was fun spending the day with my mom, no matter what we were doing. She turned on loud music while we worked, and there was always a reward at the end. Ironically, it was usually a trip to the mall to buy new things, or at least put them on layaway, but we felt we'd earned it. And sharing a sundae in a diner after the stores had closed for the night was the perfect end to our day together.

The relationship between a mother and a daughter is a unique one. And maybe mine with my mom is especially unique, since I'm a daughter *and* an only child; it seems to constantly change. There were the times I can't remember—when I was a baby and needed her to survive. Times when her approval meant everything to me, times when I couldn't stand to be in the same room with her, and times when I would cry and cry because I missed her so much. Sometimes I have felt like a sister to her, sometimes more of a friend. I've heard my father say how alike we are; I've heard her voice come out of my mouth and seen her hands when looking down at my own. We are deeply connected, and I'd say there's a chance she was probably my mom in a past life, or I was hers, if I believed in that stuff.

Here is a brief history of what I know about my mom. She was born Mollie Ann Greer. She is from Carey, Ohio. She had seven brothers and sisters and was the daughter of a social worker/farmer and a teacher. She was best friends with her sister Judy but is close to all her living siblings. When she was eleven, she was shot in the chest by her brother, who was four. It was one of those freak gun accidents you hear about. After going hunting, her older brothers had left their guns on the ground by a tree, her baby brother saw them, thought they were toys, picked one up, aimed it at my mom through the kitchen window, and pulled the trigger. The bullet missed her heart by a hair. She spent weeks in the hospital healing from her wound. She still has a scar on her boob, and here's something creepy: I have the same scar. Exactly. It really freaked my mom out when I showed her the first time. I'd include a photo of it, but I don't want to put a photo of my boob in my book. She actually never has a bad thing to say about that accident; in fact she always says she was glad it happened because that was when she realized that she wanted to be a nurse. She told me the doctors did a great job, yes, but it was the nurses who were the real heroes, and she wanted to do what they did, take care of sick people.

But, not so fast, Mollie . . . She took an eight-year detour in the convent before going to nursing school. Yeah, my mom was engaged to Jesus. She got kicked out before she took her final (marriage to Jesus) vows, but she says she has no regrets about that either because she feels like she gave her best (most potentially whorish—my words) years to the Lord until the mother superior finally kicked her out, saying she felt my mom would be better suited serving God in a more "secular" environment. You see, my mom was a bit of a rebel nun. Even then, she always loved a makeover. It was long enough ago that nuns still wore habits—and there was no such thing as casual Friday in the convent, those ladies were *covered* at all times—but that didn't stop Sister Mollie from trying to improve her fellow sisters' personal nun style. She would shave heads, give perms, and pick out new eyeglasses, and she even bought herself a red bathing suit when a local parishioner invited all the nuns to go swimming in his pool one hot afternoon. (He's no dummy. Imagine if that were today, the YouTube video . . .) Well, that episode was the last straw, as my mom explains it, and the Nun Boss basically fired my mom, but even though she was a failed nun and never got to marry God, she went home feeling as if a huge weight had been lifted off her shoulders. Apparently, she never heard a calling. She knew she didn't belong there, and she told me that every time her sister

Sister Mary Elizabeth Ann, a.k.a. Mollie Evans

Judy would come for a visit, Judy would say, "Are you ready to come home with us yet?" So, when she broke off her engagement to Jesus, my mom confessed to my grandpa that she'd always *really* wanted to go to nursing school and that was her true calling. Still to this day, she has no idea how he came up with the money, but her dad found a way to send her to a nursing school in Cleveland. Normally, I'd take this opportunity to plug the Catholic nursing school for girls she attended, but it's a parking lot now.

When she went off to college, she was poor, she had many odd jobs, she sewed her own clothes, she couldn't go home often, but she was happy. And then she met my dad and got even happier. They were fixed up on a blind date just like my husband and me! My mom wasn't even supposed to go out with him that night, her roommate was. But the roommate was sick, so she begged my mom to come in her place. I don't think it was love at first sight for them either (see "Love Not at First Sight," p. 168), but she says that they had more fun than any of the other couples they were out with that night. It didn't hurt that her boyfriend back home had recently been admitted to a mental hospital, so she didn't have anything to lose by saying yes when my father asked if he could write to her from his college in Buffalo. And he did. Every day. For two years. You'd think that there would be some special box in their basement filled with his letters, but no, that's not Mollie's style. Unless she's lying to me, she threw them all out. She claims they were boring, but, Jesus, that's over six hundred letters . . . that's prolific. Maybe they were porny, and she was nervous I'd stumble across them someday. Gross.

After the wedding came the move to Detroit. My poor mom. She spent her learning-to-keep-house years in the convent, so she had no idea how to cook or clean for her new husband. On top of that, she was afraid to drive in Detroit (because of the traffic; I don't think we had invented carjacking yet), and she didn't have any friends there. But she always blooms where she's planted and soon got promoted from regular nurse to running her unit at the hospital. She hosted fondue parties for my dad's work friends, organized scavenger hunts with other couples, and finally found herself knocked up. Depending on which of my parents you ask on what day, I was either planned or a mistake, but either way the result was the same, me!

As alike as we are, there are ways in which we are so different, and the traits we don't share are the ones that I envy in her. She is such a hard worker and is obsessed with education. After moving to Detroit, she went back to school and got a master's degree, then on to try to get a PhD. I ruined that for her, unfortunately. Stupid me. I got tired of my mom being gone during the day for work and at night when she went to class, so she eventually dropped out of the PhD program. Sorry, Mom. She didn't stop educating herself, though. She did go back to college again, at the same time as I did, and got a second master's in hospice care. And had a whole second career as a hospice nurse when I left home. I admire her ability to manage and run things. I don't have that. I am a terrible goal accomplisher and delegator. I wish she would have passed some of that down my way.

Sometimes growing up in a house with my mom felt a little like growing up in an *I Love Lucy* episode. She always tried her hardest, but there was usually some wild outcome when she would try to do things on her own. There was the year when she forgot to turn the oven on at Thanksgiving and the turkey was still frozen when we went to take it out. You're probably wondering, as many do, why she didn't check on it at all. Yeah, I know. My dad had to run out that night and find a ham at the twenty-four-hour grocery store. Or when she decided to have a surprise fourth-birthday party for me at my babysitter's house, but since it was summer vacation and all my friends were scattered all over the

Detroit area, she just had my babysitter's daughter, who was twice my age, invite her friends. So, I woke up from my nap and wandered into the living room, and there were about twelve strangers screaming *"Surprise!"* at me. I don't think I'd ever even had a birthday party before, not to mention a surprise party. Needless to say, I screamed, ran back into my babysitter's bedroom, and cried. A few years later my mom hosted a party for me at our house, and almost immediately the kids started telling me my Kool-Aid tasted weird and because of that they hated me. I ran inside to the kitchen, where my mom was making small talk with some other moms, and told her, through tears, that no one liked me anymore because my Kool-Aid was bad. Another mom tasted it and did a spit take. "Didn't you add any sugar to this?" she asked. My mom said, "No. You're supposed to add sugar? I've never made this before." Maybe Kool-Aid is different now, but back then you added about a full cup of sugar to the pitcher, and without it, it was just colored water. My dad is diabetic, so my mom just never added sugar to anything. And kids are assholes. I also remember the time she decided to bathe my bird, Sydney. We had a huge hundred-pound retriever who had a real hard-on for that bird. Well, my father and I woke up one Saturday morning to the sound of my mom screaming. This was not necessarily unusual, but still, we ran down the stairs frantically to find my dog with his mouth full of yellow feathers and my mom trying to pry it open. R.I.P., Sydney. One of my favorite Mollie moments, though, was a total *Terms of Endearment* reenactment in an ER after I broke a toe and they were taking forever. Well, those nurses got a real treat that night from my mom, who made it sound as if I were a professional ballerina with the New York City Ballet and every minute they didn't treat me was potentially career damaging and we would be suing for all my lost wages.

She would hide Christmas presents so well she would forget about them until she found them months/years later. Which was somewhat disappointing on Christmas Day, but fun when they turned up after the fact.

I'm sure all the craziness was what made my dad love her so much. There was never a dull moment, and for an engineer that's pretty awesome. If I didn't come home from school to find her in a power suit, heels, and rubber gloves pulling panty hose out of my dog's asshole, I might find a new baby grand piano in what used to be the family room but was now the music room. She's never been able to figure out how to turn on the TV or watch a DVD, but she can run an entire hospital, go to college, and find time to hit up T.J.Maxx on the way home. I admire her selflessness, energy, and positivity, and as a stepmom I hope I have some of those same traits.

She is not shy about rewarding herself for goals accomplished, and one year, when I was very young, I remember she bought herself a mink coat. I know it's not PC now to have fur, but it was four thousand degrees below zero in Detroit in the winter, and fur really is the warmest. I have such a vivid memory of riding home at night with my parents: it would be past my bedtime, and I would fall asleep on my mom's lap, my face buried in her mink coat. I know, I know, you can't let kids ride on your lap anymore, but back then it was different. I would always wake up as we pulled in to our driveway but pretend I was still sleeping, hoping that my parents wouldn't want to wake me and I could stay like that all night. Warm, my mom's arms holding me tight, smelling her perfume, and feeling the soft fur of her jacket all over my face. I have that mink coat now. I don't wear it often, I don't need to in L.A., and I worry about having an activist throw paint on me, but when I'm feeling especially Mollie-sick, I will get it out of my closet and bury my face in it. It takes me immediately back to those nights in the car with her when I felt so safe and loved. Even if I was a fender bender away from being launched out the front windshield, I wouldn't trade those car rides on my mom's lap for anything.

Anything You Can Do, I Can Do Better

IN FOURTH-ISH GRADE I WAS TAKING BALLET CLASSES, and I seemed to be getting serious about it. I don't remember exactly why my parents pulled me out of Miss Bunny's School of Dance, which was conveniently located a few miles away from our house, or if they even wanted to, but they started driving me twenty-plus minutes out of the way to the Milligan School of Ballet. And for some reason, it was decided that dance was my thing.

See, all kids had a thing, and I didn't have a thing yet. I wasn't sporty—I tried soccer once, it wasn't good. I was resentful that I had to miss morning cartoons on Saturdays. It was cold outside on those fall mornings, and I really wanted to just be home and cozy up in front of the TV while my mom made pancakes. Also, my dad was the assistant coach, which ensured that we fought a lot about soccer. I didn't want to do it, but he made me stick the season out, and then I quit.

Then there were the instruments, piano and flute to be specific. My mom was obsessed with a boy I went to grade school with, Tony Bonamici (he goes by Anthony now, or at least on the Internet he does), and he was a child piano prodigy when we were seven. I couldn't compete with that! But my mom was convinced that if I practiced more, I could play like Tony. I didn't practice, because I knew I'd never play like that kid. I don't care what Malcolm Gladwell says about ten thousand hours; if I practiced thirty thousand hours, I *still* wouldn't play like Tony. He had music in his soul. I just liked listening to my Madonna records, and practicing the piano really cut into that time for me.

There were art classes, ice-skating, swimming lessons, and I think I even signed up for hockey at one point, but the practices were at 6:00 a.m., and that wasn't a good time for me. Early and cold were both not options after failing at soccer. Clearly I was running out of time to find a thing and get good at it, so dance was sort of a last-ditch effort. I started ballet classes when I was nine years old, which in dancer years might as well be thirty-two. But I was really skinny, so I looked like a ballerina, and even if I wasn't a great dancer, sometimes it's all about looking the part. I liked dancing, I liked my dance friends (one of them had a pool), I liked all the different classes Miss Bunny offered, and it was located in a strip mall next door to a video rental store, so we usually rented a movie a few nights a week after class. This was before the days of Blockbuster. (I guess we are now in post-Blockbuster days. Weird.) So, dancing stuck and it seemed like I had finally found a thing.

Now that I'm a stepparent, I can imagine the stress my lack of a thing caused my parents. I mean, when people ask you about your kids, what do you say if they don't have a thing? "Sally is such a mellow girl; she is happy just lying on the sofa for hours." Or, "Doug was so cute watching TV all night last night." No parent really wants to say that. You want to say, "Abe hit a home run at Little League last weekend," and "Gretchen got the violin solo in *Peter and the Wolf* in her school orchestra." "Bob rescued all the hostages in *Call of Duty* last night" just doesn't cut it at company holiday parties and family reunions.

Anyway, moving dance studios to the Milligan School of Ballet was a big step for me. This was a serious ballet academy that focused on classical Russian ballet. No more modern, tap, or jazz (what is jazz dancing anyway?)—it was serious Russian ballet only from now on. It turned out I was *really* bad at classical Russian ballet, and serious classical ballerinas are (generally) total bitches. That didn't stop me from torturing myself for several years while trying to get better at it (I never did) and trying to persuade those bitches to like me (they never would). The main problem was I *looked* like I would be really good at ballet because I was so skinny. I think even my instructor Miss Karen Milligan would agree the disparity between my look and my ability was frustrating. However, I credit the time I spent on stage dancing, no matter my skill level, with giving me the confidence to try out for the high school musical and the magnet acting program as well. Well, I got cast in the chorus of the musical and made it into the acting program, somehow. It was fun, more fun than the regular high school classes. Toward the end of high school I was getting cast in some real roles in the musicals and plays. Acting was starting to feel like something I liked doing; at least I liked it better than dancing. Maybe my "thing" was changing.

Then it was time for the future, and the future comes fast in high school. One afternoon, I fell down on the concrete steps of my front porch and hurt my knee. It really wasn't all that serious of an injury, but I used it as an excuse to quit dancing so seriously. I was too scared to just quit ballet—I had put so much time and energy into it, my parents had spent so much money, and my room and bathroom were covered in ballet tchotchkes. In addition to all the time that not dancing would free up, I would have to redecorate as well. So I seized the opportunity and began an injury-induced phaseout, which was the beginning of the end of me and the Milligan School of Ballet. I was starting to like high school, I had after-school activities that were located in the actual school, and I had started to make more friends, kind of. There was one girl in particular, Marci Urbaniak. The term "frenemy" hadn't been coined yet, but the first time I heard it used, the face of Marci Urbaniak popped right into my head. Marci had already worked professionally as an actress in the Detroit area. She had head shots, and I think she'd done some commercials or maybe industrial films (which she never forgot to remind us of) by the time we met in high school. Marci and another girl named Melissa were also in the high school acting program I auditioned for. Marci and Melissa were very best friends, they made that clear, and I would only ever be a third. I was welcomed into their inner circle, but only if I understood that their friendship came first and I would never, ever be as close to either of them as they were to each other. I didn't really care, because I had my own best friend, Nicole, but she was supersmart and took the smart classes, and I needed some friends in my own classes. Besides, I'm pretty competitive by nature, so I enjoyed the challenge of seeing how close of a third I could be or if I could win one of them over. I never did. Once we all went our separate ways after high school, we quickly grew apart. Well, I did. Maybe they're still close. I hope so.

By the time we were thinking about colleges, I was at a loss. I didn't know where to go or what I wanted to do with my life. The only place I could think of was New York, but my parents said it was too far away and they wouldn't pay for school if I went there. My parents were always baiting me with tuition. The first time was when they pulled me out of private elementary school—they promised I could go back if I hated the public school, which I did, and then they changed their minds. They said the private school was too expensive and too far away. I tried again in high school, begging them to send me to a fancy private boarding school about forty-five minutes away. They said I could go there, but then I would have to pay for my own college tuition since that would eat up all their college savings. Again, I stayed in the public school. And finally, when college time came around, they conned me into staying close to home by telling me, again, that I would have to pay for myself if I went farther away. Since I can remember, all I wanted was to leave home and see the world, so I sat down with my parents and asked them seriously, how far away are we talking? What is the absolute farthest away I can go and still have you pay? Chicago was agreed upon—it was a train ride, fast flight, or a five-hour drive away, which was totally doable for a weekend if I got homesick (read: my mom missed me) or if I needed to come home for a weekend (read: laundry).

My secret fantasy was always to be a fashion designer, but I couldn't (and still can't) draw, so I didn't think I would ever get into a design school. But other than that, I had no idea what I wanted to be when I grew up. Even though I was already taking acting classes, doing school plays, and so on, it didn't occur to me there was a future in it. I just had fun doing it and I made some friends and it was a fun way to pass the time in high school until college, when I was sure I would really blossom. One day, in acting class, Marci announced that of the many theater programs she was considering for college, she was auditioning for an acting program at a college in Chicago and it was so exclusive that they only accepted 10 percent of the people who auditioned for it. Marci implied that an acting dilettante like myself would never get in and shouldn't try because it was only for those who were really serious about acting. Well, Marci was right: I wasn't serious about acting, but I was serious about Chicago, and I wasn't really good at anything else yet. When I got home from school that night, I told my mom about Marci's latest brag and that she thought it was too exclusive for me to get into . . . blah blah blah.

My mom wasn't having it. She got all fierce and said, "No one tells my daughter she can't get in anywhere."

"Mom, the audition is this weekend. Today's Tuesday. There's no way I will get all the paperwork and crap together in time."

"Just let me figure that out. Start working on a monologue. We're going to Chicago on Friday night."

Mollie Evans can be really intense when she needs to be, she rarely takes no for an answer, and, miraculously, in a world before the Internet and e-mail, she managed to get me applied and registered for the auditions that weekend at the Theatre School at DePaul University (thank you, magical fax machines). I did some weird monologue from a Jean-Claude van Itallie play called "The Serpent," and when I finished, Ric Murphy, my future first-year acting teacher, asked if I had another monologue, something a little more mainstream. I didn't. But I lied and made one up off the top of my head from *To Kill a Mockingbird*. What did I care? I wasn't even going to go to this school anyway, but my competitive spirit kicked in again, and I *was* going to at least get accepted to this program, whether I went there or not. I was going to get a letter of acceptance in my mailbox no matter what and immediately show it to Marci.

And guess what? I did! *I* was one of 10 percent of the kids who auditioned that year to make it in. But now I had to deal with the question of whether I would go or not. It was Chicago, it was acting, I would get a bachelor's degree, which seemed to be really important to my parents after all the money they were about to spend, and I had a girlfriend there, Amy, who was a year older and studying smart-people things, so, built-in friend. The only snag was Marci. She got in too, and if she went there, it would ruin my total-reinvention plan, where I got to leave behind the old Judy and start fresh where no one knew me, so I waited to find out what she was going to do. She had auditioned for a few different schools—I didn't. I applied to two crappy backups but wasn't as excited about anything else now that Chicago was a real possibility. Thankfully, Marci got accepted to a musical theater program that she liked better than the plain old acting one at DePaul, so she went there. I accepted my acceptance and got ready to learn how to act.

The Theatre School at DePaul University is a four-year conservatory program that focuses on acting entirely. You take a few academic classes, but they are kind of designed for us to pass, like the ones athletes take. And then you act. You act all day and all night basically. You take your acting classes during the day, and at night you are either on the crew of a play or in a play. It's really time-consuming, and I had no idea what I was getting myself into when I started. I remember thinking that I would probably transfer after my first year because I wasn't going to be an actress and I was getting no real education, but it was fun. And it was such a small program. There were only a hundred students in our first year, divided into four classes, and after both first year and second you had to be invited back. They cut our class in half after the first year and then in half again after the second. If you were in danger of not getting invited back, you were put on warning. Your main acting teacher would take you into his or her office and tell you you were being warned. They would tell you why and what you had to do in order to be invited back. Once you made it to your third year, you were home free and didn't have to worry anymore. I was on warning both years. I was told I had to work on my voice. The quality and the accent. I had a very distinctive midwestern accent. In the Midwest we have a specific way of speaking, it's nasally, and I often ended my sentences with an up glide? So everything sounded like a question? When I was talking? And I guess that annoyed the faculty? So they told me to stop? Or I would get kicked out of school? Yeah. I guess they were right. It's as annoying to write as it is to listen to. As for my vocal quality, I think in order to be onstage and be heard, you really have to project from your belly and not sound as if you're shouting. It's hard and I'm still pretty shitty at it, but I work on it when I need to, and the theater school taught me how to do it.

Luckily, I never got asked to leave acting school, and I never transferred. I just stayed. Maybe I was lazy, but I was having fun. I loved living with my roommates, I loved Chicago, I loved having a small group of people to work with every day, and after a few years I started to really love acting. I think what I'm really saying is I owe my career to my education, and I owe my education to Marci Urbaniak. OK, my parents paid, and my mom was the one who got me the last-minute audition, and I was the one who went to my classes (even on the day it was minus-eighty degrees outside and I cried walking to school and my tears froze on my face), but if it wasn't for my first frenemy telling me I couldn't hack it, I wouldn't be where I am today, sitting in bed writing a book about myself.

Carey Christmas

middle of Ohio, or central Ohio, as I have heard my relatives call it. My mother grew up there, and a majority of her side of the family still lives there. My parents moved back several years ago. They bought a cute house on a farm. They didn't buy *a* farm; they bought a house *on* a farm. It's the best of both worlds if you ask me. They get to be surrounded by farm but without having to actually grow anything. We went to Carey all the time when I was a kid. It was a two-hour drive from where we lived in the suburbs of Detroit. It's a rural town that had a population of about two thousand people, although it may be larger now. It's filled with my family members, and we're super fertile (my mom warned me of this when I left home for college). If you've ever seen the TV show *Friday Night Lights*, it's that kind of town, where everything revolves around the high school. It's very Norman Rockwell meets recession. There's one main street, a few bars, a few restaurants, a drugstore, supermarket, library, Ford dealership, and some various lodges for Elks or Moose (not the animals), a giant famous Catholic church, and even a nine-hole golf course made out of an old cow pasture. Since my mom's side of the family was so giant, there was a special Greer family Christmas party every year, in mid-December, so that the whole Greer clan could celebrate together, like a mini family reunion but in my aunt's house instead of a park. We called it the Carey Christmas, and it was a big deal when I was a kid. My aunt would hire a local guy to dress up in a Santa suit, and he would show up halfway through the day. Everyone would gather around with their cameras, and he would have a giant bag of toys, one for each grandkid with his or her name on it. As Santa pulled out each gift from his giant bag, he would call out the name on the present, and we would have to go up and sit on Santa's lap and tell him that we were good little boys and girls and ask for what we wanted for real Christmas. A photo would be taken, Santa would give us our gift, and he would move on to the next grandkid.

Even at a young age, sitting on this stranger's lap bothered me a little. I don't remember ever believing in Santa, so the idea that I had to do this every year felt false. I *wanted* to believe in Santa; I just didn't. You can't help what you believe and what you don't. I blame my mother's handwriting. Every time there was a gift under our Christmas tree from Santa, it was clearly my mother's handwriting. I think my parents knew better than to have my dad do it; as an engineer, he basically used graphing equipment to handwrite anything, but my mom's was just as recognizable, just in a beautiful schoolteacher kind of way. Maybe they didn't want to have to buy so many different gifts, they kept it simple and just stuck to the main ones, none of the stocking stuffer bullshit. Or perhaps they didn't want to give some fake dude all the credit for all the gifts they spent their hard-earned money on during the holidays. Maybe they wanted all the glory, and honestly I can't really blame them. I would be pissed if my kids were screaming out someone else's name on the second-happiest day of the year (I considered the day *The Wizard of Oz* was on TV the happiest day of the year).

Actually, fuck Santa. Sorry, that got dark, but I do kind of wish I had believed in him. It seemed so fun for all my friends, and I would have loved to have that dramatic memory of the day I found out there was no Santa. I didn't get that milestone, so now I have to rely on celebrity divorces for that kind of shock and betrayal. I have no memory of any gift I ever got from Carey Christmas Santa, but I have photos of myself all the way up to the age of seventeen sitting on his lap. I now think that might have been too old to be sitting on a stranger's lap, even if I was surrounded by a hundred family members and a gun case filled with rifles was in the next room.

There are other things about Carey that I remember fondly. I was very best friends with my cousin Mandy, who grew up there. We joked that we were the city mouse and the country mouse. She would come visit me, and we would go to the mall, and I

On Santa's lap, age 17

would visit her, and we would feed sheep and play in the crick (aka creek) behind the barn. It was fun to run around their farm and play with the little goats and barn cats. They used to have pigs too, which I am so mad at myself for not taking full advantage of. I'd love to play with a little piglet. It's harder than you'd think to find a piglet to play with for an afternoon in Los Angeles. I watched cows get slaughtered in the snow outside my aunt Deanna's kitchen window. I saw the dead deer that my cousins and uncles would kill during hunting season, and I'd eat it all too. That's pretty good for a girl growing up outside Detroit. I didn't think much of it at the time, because it was just what we did, but as I look back, hanging out with my family on farms in Small Town, U.S.A., was awesome. Summers were the best. We would ride our bikes all over, catch lightning bugs in the fields at night and put them in Mason jars with holes punched in the top, swim in my aunt's pond, and sleep with the windows open all night, listening to the sound of the crickets. The sound of crickets is a major player in my noise machine lineup. It makes me feel like the little city mouse in the country again, and when I hear them, I can still smell the faintest whiff of cow manure as I drift off to sleep.

The only thing about Carey, Ohio, that I remember being scary, besides the year I read *In Cold Blood*, was the church, Our Lady of Consolation Basilica and National Shrine. I like old churches—I like to visit them when I travel, probably because they remind me of OLC. I think they are cool and creepy, and they remind me of scary devil movies, and this one is no exception. I grew up going to Mass there when I was a kid visiting Carey. It is huge, like Italy-church huge. And old, not Italy-church old, but still, *old*. It has all the makings of a great devil movie set. A huge choir loft, spiral staircases, many entrances and exits, giant stained-glass windows, a huge organ, a massive altar with hundreds of red glass

candles of different sizes burning 24/7, a life-size Jesus statue
lying in a coffin on one side of the altar (stage right) complete
with cuts and a crown of thorns, and, the pièce de résistance, on
the other side of the altar (stage left) a statue of Our Lady herself,
holding the baby Jesus and a scepter. It is claimed that miracles
have happened at this shrine and that they started in 1875, when
the gift of the statue of Our Lady was carried a hundred miles
on foot in a processional, from St. Nicholas Church in French-
town, Ohio, once construction of the shrine was completed. A
storm raged throughout central Ohio during the processional that
day, but not a drop touched the Mary statue. A miracle! And ever
since, people have traveled from near and far to get a few drops
(or a bottleful) of the holy water that runs out of a tap on the
side of the church. When I got a little older and was allowed
to watch scary devil movies, I realized that this echoey building of faith, art, and history could provide a lot more than just
comfort for the tired, weary, and faithful. It could be a place of
paranormal murder, and I suddenly started to like going to church
a lot more. I pretended that a gust of wind was going to slam the
carved wooden doors shut and lock us all in. That all at once the
candles would flicker, extinguish, then light again! I pretended
that no one was in the choir loft when there was singing and
organ music. But the best part of all was the basement. Because
there were so many miracles related to OLC and churches like
to show off to their parishioners and the Vatican, there are glass
boxes that line the perimeter of this basement prayer room, filled
with discarded crutches, braces, helmets, gurneys, cabinet after
cabinet of devices that were no longer required by the infirm. I'm
sorry, but it's creepy. The few cabinets that don't store proof of
miracles house the many dresses of Our Lady. Oh yes, she has
more dresses than I do. She's fickle and gets to change clothes
depending on the holiday, time of year, if she gets dirty. I don't

know the ins and outs of why/how/when Mary gets a new dress, but it's really impressive to see the racks and racks of little outfits. I've always been a bit jealous.

I eventually got more interested in my real life than my fantasy life while sitting through Mass in Carey. The altar boys became better eye candy than the stained-glass windows (the altar boys who weren't related to me, that is; sometimes I had to ask my mom if one was a first or second cousin, just to be sure). And when I went off to college, I stopped making it back for the Carey Christmas. Now that I'm all grown up, working and traveling so much, I hardly make it back there at all; usually my parents come out to see me. But in a lot of ways, I consider Carey one of my homes. I never felt like I totally belonged there, because I wasn't cut from its cloth, but I was the next-best thing, and when I do make it back, I always make sure to go to the shrine. I'm not a practicing Catholic anymore, but I like to light a candle anyway and think about one of the many miracles in my life: Carey, Ohio.

My First Pube

A THIRTEENTH BIRTHDAY IS A VERY IMPORTANT BIRTH-
day for a young girl—well, it was for me. I was finally going to
become a teenager. My dad told me that when I turned thirteen,
I could buy the teen mags at the drugstore, like *Teen Beat*, *Tiger
Beat*, and basically anything with boys on the cover and the word
"beat" in the title. Being thirteen meant I was three years closer
to being sixteen, which was just two years away from being eighteen, and then, before I knew it, I would be twenty-one, which
to me meant I was a grown-up! Once I turned thirteen, I was
sure my hair would start to straighten, I would grow boobs, and
Jeff Hunt, my adolescent crush (read: obsession), would fall in
love with me. Spoiler alert: none of that happened. I don't even
remember if I was obsessing about pubic hair or not at the time.
I had one goal and one goal only: BOOBS. Pubic hair you could
lie about; boobs you could not. It was obvious when girls stuffed
their bras—besides, what do you do in the summer at pool parties, assuming you get invited to them? How do you stuff a bathing suit? Duct tape and a couple of overripe plums? And if you
can't figure out how to stuff a bathing suit, how do you explain
your sudden flatness? Weight loss? I needed boobs! Ones that

would make boys (Jeff Hunt) notice me and offer to buy me a Slurpee. I was convinced that if I could just get a boy (Jeff Hunt) to walk with me to 7-Eleven and buy me a Slurpee, I could win him over with my charm and quick wit, but I needed the boobs to get the ball rolling.

That summer I turned thirteen, my parents and I were going on our summer vacation, which was always a road trip to somewhere boring—sorry, "serene." I still don't understand why we never went anywhere far away enough that we had to take an airplane. We never flew anywhere. Not even Disney in Orlando (is it "world" or "land"? I will never remember because MY PARENTS NEVER TOOK ME THERE!!!). We went to northern Michigan (a lot), Iowa, North Carolina, Wisconsin, and places like that. I slept in the car a lot on those trips. To this day, anytime I am in the car for an extended period of time, I get so tired I can hardly keep my eyes open. Even if I'm just running errands or driving to an audition, if the traffic is particularly terrible and I'm in the car forever, I will have to pull over and close my eyes for a few minutes—it's not safe to drive like that. My mom said that when I was really little, in my car seat, I would dress and undress my Barbies between naps. When I got older, I read, and read, and read. Thank God I never got carsick! Sometimes my parents would let me bring a cousin or friend to keep me company during our trip and probably to keep me out of their hair. But often I would just go alone.

So, this particular year, we went to visit my mom's cousin, who I'd never met, in Wisconsin. Her family owned a lodge, and we were going to stay there for the night on our way to a cabin on a lake in Minnesota that was owned by my father's uncle, who I'd *also* never met. When we arrived at the lodge, I thought it was real fancy. It reminded me of where Baby and her family stayed in *Dirty Dancing*, minus the hot, oversexed dancers. There was a main building that had hotel rooms and the dining room, and then there were little cabins and clusters of buildings that had several hotel rooms in each one, like mini strip malls. They were scattered around the grounds, with trees everywhere and little paths connecting everything. I remember being so excited because I had my own room, and I *never* got my own room. I thought it was appropriate that I finally get a room of my own because I was a day away from being thirteen, practically an adult, voting was just around the corner. That night, we went to dinner in the dining room of the main building with the cousin, and I remember my parents were drinking wine and decided to stay later than I wanted to, which was fine by me because I needed to be alone anyway to say good-bye to my preteen self and hello to the new teenage me. So I went back to my room alone (another sign that I was fully grown up). I decided an evening of solitary pampering was the perfect way to celebrate this rite of passage. I mean, I had my own room, and in the movies when women had their own hotel rooms, they always took hot bubble baths, applied lots of colored lotions, wrapped their hair in a towel, turban style, and danced around lip-synching to a lady-power song. If this was how independent women were supposed to behave, I thought I should get started.

I used the mini shampoo to make my bubble bath. This never works for long, if at all, but since no one told me I'd have my own room, I didn't come prepared with the proper bath supplies. I didn't come close to getting as many bubbles going as they do in the movies, but it was pampering enough. It wasn't until I was drying off, pre-lip-synch dance, that I noticed it. One curly black hair stuck to the skin of my pelvis. One hair. At first I almost barfed, thinking it was someone else's hair left over from the previous occupant of the tub, but when I tried to remove it with the towel, it hurt. And that was when I realized it wasn't a stranger's pube but my own! My very own pubic hair! I got excited because I knew in my heart it was a sign. My life was turning around. I wasn't going to be flat and ugly anymore. My hair was going to grow. I was going to start looking more and more like Alyssa Milano every day. But most of all, I was going to be OK. I would have friends. I would be popular. Jeff Hunt would fall in love with me. It was all starting, and now I had proof because of that one little black curly hair. I think this ecstatic feeling is why I still have no idea why women shave/pluck/wax off all their pubic hair. It was a curly miracle to me, that night in the woods in Wisconsin, and I remember all it symbolized. Why would I get rid of it? It meant something—mostly that I wasn't a total freak, but still, it meant something. I liked it. It made me feel like a woman, not like the girl I was so desperate to leave behind on my vacation, but the woman I would morph into as the summer ended, and, surely, by the first day of high school I would walk through the halls, my metamorphosis complete. The crowds of upperclassmen would part and make room for this mysterious new student who was literally bursting with confidence (when I say "bursting," I mean my boobs would be about to pop my shirt open). I fell asleep with this fantasy dancing around in my head.

The next thing I remember is maybe the scariest moment in my life so far. I was sound asleep, and there was pounding on the door and my mom was yelling for me to wake up. When I opened the door, she was standing there, talking very slowly and deliberately, so calm, in fact, that it was eerie. She said that I needed to run up to the lodge and call an ambulance as fast as I could, that my dad was really sick and I had to go, now, quickly, or he would die. My dad has diabetes—not the fat kind but the kind you get when you're a kid and have forever. It was a major part of our lives and the source of most of my parents' arguments, mostly because when my dad's blood sugar got too low, he turned into a total asshole. Not his fault, but it was pretty obvious when he was low, and you can't really get that mad at him for it. But still, no one likes an asshole.

I immediately took off running on the path to the lodge. It was so dark that I couldn't see a thing, but I just kept running through the woods until I finally saw the lights from the main building ahead of me. Once I got there, I didn't know what to do. Even though it was the middle of the night, I thought somehow there would be someone there, waiting to help me. There was no one. The front door was unlocked. I ran inside and started screaming at the top of my lungs, "HELP!! HELP! SOMEBODY HELP ME!!!" I screamed and cried and screamed louder, but nothing worked. No one came. Just then my mom ran into the lobby. She ran right behind the desk and grabbed the phone and called 911. Like she had been there a million times, like she worked there. How did she know to do that? How did she know exactly where to go and what to do? In that moment I felt worse than I had ever felt in my life. How stupid was I? Why didn't I think of that? Of course the phone, of course 911. I'm the worst daughter, and if my dad died, it would be my fault. My mom told me to wait in front of the building for the ambulance and show them where our rooms were, she was going to go back to my dad. It seemed like the trees got bigger while I was standing there, the sky got darker, and there was no such thing as time anymore, just darkness and quiet. I made a million promises that night, to whatever was out there, that I would do anything if my dad was OK. I apologized to the universe for everything bad I had ever done and pleaded that my dad shouldn't be punished because I was a terrible person. And then I noticed something in the dark moving toward me—a shadow, and it was getting larger and larger. It had to be a bear, I thought. I was in the middle of the woods, it was nighttime, I needed to be punished for not thinking to dial 911, and I had just admitted to the gods that it was probably my fault this was happening at all for having stolen Amy's hamburger gum at her birthday party six years ago and lying about practicing piano, among my other sins. It was clearly a karma bear coming for me. This was the moment in my life when I learned something very valuable about my intrinsic nature. You've heard of the fight-or-flight response? Well, I learned that I am not a fight-or-flight type of person—I am a paralyzed-frozen-in-fear type of person. I froze. I froze hard. I don't even think my heart was beating as the shadow, obviously a bear, stretched out longer and longer and got bigger and bigger, as though the shadow itself were reaching for my toes, and then I heard a sound, the tiniest little squeak. Wait, why was it squeaking? Would a bear squeak? Was it . . . could it have been . . . a meow? And then there was another squeak, and then another, and finally the creature presented itself. My karma bear was a kitten, a small, fuzzy, dirty, squeaky kitten. I burst into tears; I couldn't handle this. I wasn't ready to be a grown-up, pubic hair or not. There was still no ambulance, I had no idea what was happening to my dad, the kitten was now rubbing back and forth against my legs, and all I seemed to be capable of was standing there and crying. I wasn't blessed with a fight response, I have no flight instincts whatsoever, but where I really excel is in the lesser-known stand-and-cry reaction. It hasn't been as extensively researched by psychologists, but it's a thing. I'm a living, breathing example of it.

When the paramedics arrived, I pulled it together long enough to lead them down the path to my dad. My mom yelled for them, telling them what was happening and using a lot of medical terms. I don't know what they did to him in that room; there wasn't enough space for me to be in there as well, so I just waited outside. I heard them saying his name a lot and asking him several questions that my mother answered, but they seemed less interested in her words and more interested in getting my dad to talk. They eventually loaded us all into the ambulance, and again there wasn't enough room, so I had to sit on my mother's lap in the passenger seat. We sped down this dark road toward the hospital, slamming on the brakes once to avoid hitting a deer in the middle of the road. Every time I hear the phrase "a deer in the headlights," the image of that deer face from that night in Wisconsin pops into my head. When we got to the hospital, I sat by myself in the ER waiting room, listening to my dad throw up in an exam room down the hall. I don't know why he was throwing up, but it was impressively loud, and I felt proud and relieved. He wouldn't be barfing with that much power and volume if he was dying. No way, that was the retching of a soon-to-be-healthy adult male, and when the nurse behind the desk looked at me with pity, I announced proudly that that was my dad barfing.

The next day was my thirteenth birthday, and even though I felt sure my dad was going to be fine, I knew that everything would be different. And it was. My mom and dad were on lockdown. Our diets changed. My parents stopped drinking, blaming the wine they had that night for my dad's blood sugar dropping so low while he was sleeping. My father started checking his blood sugar so many times a day that all of his fingers grew calluses all over them. He started giving himself five shots a day of insulin, and he wasn't allowed to just have a Snickers when he got low, which sucked for me because I could always count on my dad having candy on him. Now it was just glucose tablets, juice boxes, and oranges.

When I started high school that fall, I looked the same, I acted the same, my hair was the same, Jeff Hunt didn't fall in love with me, and I wasn't bursting with anything. It's really hard to be mysterious if no one is paying attention to you in the first place. It was OK, though. I was happy with my few friends, and since I was alone a lot, I learned to be independent. And I did change that summer. I learned that sometimes good things can come from terrible events. My dad got really sick that night, but because of it he got so much healthier overall. Life is precious and can change so fast. One second you can be admiring your first pube, the next second listening to the beautiful sounds of your dad's vomiting echoing through a hospital hallway.

Waiting Tables Makes You a Bitter Person

waiting tables, and service industry jobs in general, make you a better person. I've had several jobs in the service industry. I got my start when I was fifteen at a "Greek" chain restaurant in the local mall called Olga's Kitchen. I used quotation marks around "Greek" because it had a Greek name, was named after a Greek lady, and served Greek salad, but other than that the menu consisted entirely of American variations on the gyro, unless they serve Chinese chicken gyros in Greece. (Maybe they do! I have never been to Greece, so I can't really say for sure.) I started working at the cash register at the front, seating people, cashing them out, and selling these crazy-huge delicious muffins out of the muffin case. Whatever muffin image is in your brain right now, triple it and add a bigger top. They were gorgeous, and many customers would come just to have coffee and a muffin. Again, not super sure they serve muffins in Greece, but no one in Livonia was complaining about the authenticity of our menu. The muffins were our secret weapon at Olga's Kitchen because they could be used to bribe unhappy customers into submission. If someone was disappointed with how a gyro was prepared or the temperature of the soup, all we had to do was deliver one of these Fiat-size muffins to his table and say, "We are so sorry you weren't totally satisfied with your meal today. Here, breakfast is on us tomorrow morning." We'd add in a huge fake smile with manufactured undertones of sympathy for his hard life, and he would beg to pay his whole check. Free muffin = secret weapon, if only life were that easy everywhere else.

Once I turned sixteen and paid my dues as a hostess/cashier, I was promoted to the coveted position of waitress. That was where you made the real money. Jo was our head waitress. She was one of those people who could have been thirty or sixty—it was impossible to tell—but she was a classy broad, I could make her laugh, and she helped me out when I was in the weeds, needed a break, or was having an emotional breakdown in the back. Jo had worked there forever and seemed to like it. I think they tried to make her a manager at one point, but she wasn't into it, because she made more money, had less responsibility, and could take more smoke breaks as a waitress. Plus, she had seniority, so she didn't have to do the hard shit like mop the floors or clean the bathrooms. Well, maybe she was supposed to, but we respected her too much to let her. She looked out for the rest of us girls, and I was always happy when I showed up for work and she was just getting there too, because that meant it would be a fun shift. She taught me to work hard and do a good job but not take it all too seriously. After all, it was Olga's Kitchen, not the UN.

In addition to our monochromatic, wrinkle-free polyester uniforms, we all had name tags made with our names on them. But if we forgot ours, there was a drawer under the cash register filled with random leftovers from previous employees that we could just grab. It was exciting to have a different name for a shift. Some days I was a Carol, sometimes a Nancy. I was a way better waitress as a Carol than as a Nancy, though. When I was Nancy, all I cared about was smoking on the upside-down bucket by the back door and finishing my shift. As Carol, I was much more concerned with customer satisfaction and restaurant cleanliness. It was ultimately a bad idea to wear another name tag because when a customer called out my "name," I wouldn't notice, and therefore I'd walk right by. On those days my tips usually reflected this bad choice.

Other highlights at Olga's included flirting with the kitchen staff, who were either seniors in a nearby high school or attending the local community college, and free food. We weren't allowed to have free gyros, but sometimes the cooks would make one for us and lie about it being a mistake. We were, however, allowed to eat all the pita, salad, and soup we wanted. I was especially clever with my free pita and salad. I made salad-stuffed gyros for myself every day and dipped them in the soup. I mean, the soup was hot and *free*, and I especially loved the way the free part tasted. To this day, I blame Olga's Kitchen for my obsessive-compulsive need for feta cheese on a daily basis. I don't think I'd ever had feta cheese until that job, and now I can't give it up.

I loved working at Olga's and acquired some real life skills in my time there. I learned how to smoke cigarettes, how to make a bathroom look clean without actually cleaning it, the art of playing dumb, and how to just add more lettuce to a Greek salad when the customer sent it back complaining there was too much dressing. It was an easy job, and thankfully, in the Midwest in the late 1990s, there wasn't the influx of food allergies that there is today or extreme dietary restrictions. Not everyone was a gluten-free vegan. No one cared where their cow or egg came from, and the letters *GMO* didn't exist in that order. People ate their BBQ pork gyro, got a muffin to go, and went back to shopping.

My next food service job was in a restaurant called I Tre Merli in Chicago. I was a freshman in college and was working at Express in a strip mall near campus. I hated it, but they worked around my schedule, it was money, and I needed that. I had been banned from working the floor for telling customers the truth about how the clothes looked on them and had been delegated to the stockroom, where I was in charge of attaching those safety tags to each and every garment before it went out on the floor. My manager had a nervous breakdown one day when she found a pile of security tags in the corner of a dressing room after a thief had pried them off the clothes. I think she secretly blamed me for those tags being ripped off, but she had no proof, so she just gave me the silent treatment, which I preferred anyway. I also didn't mind the stockroom, because our Express shared a storage room with the men's equivalent, Structure, and there was a guy who worked there who looked exactly like Kyle MacLachlan, a.k.a. Agent Dale Cooper from *Twin Peaks*, and since I didn't think I'd ever get a date with Kyle MacLachlan, this guy would do. There was a radio in the back that only got one golden oldies station. I learned all the words to "Leader of the Pack," even the spoken-word section. Well, despite my TV-character look-alike crush working next door, and my conviction that I could win a Guinness world record for the most times listening to the song "My Girl" during a six-hour window, I was not very committed to my job.

One day in the spring, when I was riding my bike to Express, I heard two guys revving their motorcycles, and when I looked over at them, one called out to me and motioned for me to come over. I did. In hindsight, I see that this was not a smart move, but it was daytime and they had motorcycles and they were cute and they had motorcycles . . . The one who yelled to me was named Lionel, and he told me I should come to their restaurant when I was finished working. They needed a new waitress, and I should meet the manager, Alistair. I hated Express and had already gotten Agent Cooper look-alike's phone number, so I was really just looking for an excuse to quit. After work I rode my bike to the restaurant. It was in a very hip part of town, although I had to ride my bike through the projects to get there. I saw what I was getting myself into. That place was fancy. It was like nothing I'd ever seen before—rich people in their late twenties, early thirties, seated shoulder to shoulder, wearing black and drinking wine and martinis. And it was so crowded! People were waiting out on the sidewalk to get in; the bartender looked like a supermodel. I immediately felt totally out of place in my white T-shirt, plaid miniskirt, and white Keds. When Lionel found the manager, Alistair took one look at me and said, "Oh, dear. How old are you?" I answered him honestly and replied, "Eighteen." He said, "No, you're twenty-one. Come in tomorrow at 11:00 a.m. You'll start on lunches and Wendy will train you." And that was it. I had my next restaurant gig. I was in way over my head, and I knew it right away. I didn't know how to open a bottle of wine. I didn't know anything about fine dining. I wasn't sure what half the food on the menu was, and everyone seemed so much older than me. When I think back on how old they must have been, they were young too, but I felt so immature around them. Everyone was so beautiful and experienced. They all drank a lot and did drugs. I drank and smoked weed now and then, but in a college way. This was different, and even though it was just a couple miles away from my campus, it was another world. We were a team, we pooled our tips and went out to nightclubs together after work, and then, when the nightclubs closed, we would go back to the restaurant, open it up, and hang out some more. We would listen to music and sit on the bar and drink until the sun came up, and then we would all take cabs home in the sunlight. We were like a little dysfunctional family, and we took care of each other, I thought. Years later I found out that everyone was cheating on everyone and stealing everything from everyone, but at the time I felt like I had something that everyone at school didn't have—an exciting life outside class. Acting wasn't yet everything to me, and I was still planning on leaving school and getting a real education at some point, but time was passing and I was having fun. But like everything, it had to end at some point. And finally the restaurant slowed down. Alistair left for London, another trendy place opened up where all the black-clad Chicagoans started waiting for hours for a table, and I decided to focus on school, finally.

It took a while before I got another restaurant job, but this time it was at a nightclub called Stardust. It was a huge warehouse-looking place with several levels, several different rooms, a lot of dark velvet draped everywhere, and very dim lighting. It was downtown, and my friend Marcia (the beautiful supermodel bartender from I Tre Merli) got me the job. I was hired to be a cocktail waitress, but it was an impossible job, and I knew immediately I wasn't pushy enough to make it through the crowd of sweaty dancers to deliver drinks. People would bump me and I'd spill, customers would move away from where they had ordered so I couldn't find them, and as soon as I would find them, they would order another round. I felt like Sisyphus from the ancient Greek myth, but instead of having to push a boulder up a hill, I had to deliver seven vodka cranberries to the same seven girls, over and over, forever. No way. I just didn't have it in me. After a few hours of this, I found my manager hiding in the office and told her I had to quit immediately. Turns out it was my lucky day because the coat check girl had just OD'd (not in a dead way, just in a stomach-pump kind of way) and my manager wanted to know if I would be willing to check coats for a few nights. It was actually a really hard job, and after my first night doing it, I understood why someone would need to self-medicate during a shift. There were so many coats I had to crawl on my hands and knees underneath the racks and come up in the middle to try to see the tickets on the hangers. Luckily, I didn't mind crawling through coats as much as through gyrating humans, and the previous coat check girl never came back, so the job became mine. I lost a coat almost every night that winter, and the club owner was always trying to fire me, but it never took. This was, after all, Chicago during the winter, so there were *a lot* of coats. And they were mostly black leather. Tip: if you don't want your coat to get lost in a nightclub coat check, don't wear a black leather coat. Get a pink one. Or red. Or anything that is memorable, because here is a fact: You *will* lose your ticket. You just will. And when you come to me all drunk at the end of the night with no ticket, telling me it's a black leather jacket, I simply cannot help you. I won't help you. Another little-known fact about the coat check is that it is where the (no offense) losers hang out. We have no way of escaping. We work in a black hole with no back door and nowhere to hide. I can lie and say I have to organize the coatroom behind me, and honestly I will be doing just that, even if I don't have to. I get it, coat check girls are less intimidating than bartenders—bartenders are hot and they have a lot of alcohol behind them. We're just guarding leather, and we get busy in the beginning of the night and at the end of the night, but for the middle bits we're just standing there too. Last tip, don't wear a scarf, hat, or gloves to a nightclub; just don't bring your winter accessories at all. You will never see those items again. There is no way to really deal with accessories back there, I tried to stuff them in a sleeve, but honestly, they're never going to stay there. Just leave them at home.

Once the winter was over, there wasn't much use for me in the coatroom, so I dabbled at the door for a minute. I was the girl on the stool in front of the door, holding the clipboard with the VIP list on it. I was terrible at this because I just wanted to let everyone in, and apparently I was supposed to be taking tips from people waiting in line and sharing them with the bouncers, but I didn't know, no one told me, so the bouncers got pissed, and I eventually got moved to the box. The box is where I sat and would take the cover and stamp people's hands when they paid and came in. It was the most boring of all jobs because it never ended and I was sort of forgotten about, I would get thirsty or have to pee really bad, but there was no one around to cover for me, so I would just sit there and squirm until I could flag down a fellow Stardust team member. One of the security guys asked me once if I was stealing money from the drawer, and I nearly choked on my own saliva. "No way!" I told him. "I would never do that!" He told me, totally deadpan, I was stupid and everyone skimmed off the top, that it was expected and I was an asshole if I didn't. I had been raised to believe that I was an asshole if I *did* steal, so this was really hard for me to wrap my brain around. The longer I worked there, the more it made sense. It was a nightclub, not a children's hospital. I guessed that the owners weren't looking to run a completely legit business, or wouldn't they open a Subway franchise or something? I wasn't getting paid much to sit on the stool all night, so maybe I could at least slip some cab fare in my bra or something? I was starting to buy my justification argument. I had taken home my fair share of unclaimed cashmere scarves and gloves from my previous Stardust post. Isn't that kind of the same thing? Yes, it kind of is. If a twenty-dollar bill just *happened* to fall on the floor while I was taking money that night, and I just *happened* to pick it up and forget to put it in the drawer, and I only did it once a night for my cab ride home at 5:00 a.m., when no girl should be on the streets waiting for a bus or train, wasn't I actually doing the nightclub a favor? I was saving them the headache of trying to find my replacement while I was recovering in the hospital from a potential mugging. Yes, taking money would make me a team player! I was going to do it—I was ready to break the law in the name of private business owners everywhere. What I didn't anticipate were the immediate pangs of guilt I would experience. Literally, the minute after I tucked the bill into my knee-high boot, I was doubled over with cramps. I had no idea how to steal money. Just taking a twenty-dollar bill and stuffing it in my pocket seemed too on the nose. I needed to be stealthy—I needed to remember one of the millions of scenes I had seen in movies where girls were undercover and sneaky and cool, but I was drawing a blank. My method of stealing goes as follows: drop a twenty on the floor and leave it there for about three hours, obsess over it being on the floor, begin mild cramping in abdominal area, drop hand stamp on ground near twenty, bend over to pick up hand stamp, cramps worsen, pick up hand stamp and twenty, slip twenty into knee-high boot, sit back on chair, cramps hit a ten on one-to-ten pain scale, wait for what seems like days for someone to check on me, cramps almost debilitating, the second I see another employee I yell for that person to cover for me, bolt to the bathroom, jump the line of drunk girls, get in stall, no time to wipe down seat, and do something that no one wants to ever do (or smell) in a nightclub bathroom. A thief, I am not. I literally don't have the stomach for it.

I did use my dirty money for a cab ride home that night, although in retrospect I should have left it in the bathroom attendant's tip jar—she had a thankless job and no stealing opportunities to speak of. I never stole again, and shortly after I got promoted to bartender. I started working at the downstairs bar, in a more quiet, lounge-type room. I made a lot of money for a twenty-one-year-old, and the hours were perfect for doing theater. I only worked weekends and didn't have to be there until 11:00 p.m., so I could do a play and then head to work. The weekends were long, but I had a direct line to Diet Coke at my fingertips, I was making my rent and still able to act, what more did I need?

I was lucky, and once I moved to L.A., I didn't have to get another job besides acting. But I wouldn't trade my previous jobs for anything. They played a major part in the person I am today. I firmly believe that everyone should have to work in the food service industry at least once in their lives. Like joining the army in Israel, when all Americans turn eighteen, a mandatory year of waiting tables. Yes, you'll have your bitter moments. You will cry during a shift; you will snap at your co-workers, customers, and boss. You will eat combinations of food you would never admit to now, some of it off the plates of strangers, you'll learn to roll silverware in your sleep, go through more bottles of Febreze than shampoo, you'll learn swear words in other languages, but ultimately it will make you a better person, or at least a bigger tipper.

★ 2 B

MY COLLEGE GRADUATION GIFT FROM MY PARENTS
was a car. I don't remember when my mom and dad decided on
that as a gift, and I don't know why I felt I needed one when I was
living in Chicago, which had amazing public transportation, but
that was what was decided and that was what I was going to get.
I'd made it through four years of acting school, and I deserved a
reward. Since my dad worked for Ford Motor Company and we
got an awesome employee discount (in fact, we still do!), our family has always bought Fords. My first car was also the first exception, since I got a Dodge Charger when I turned sixteen. It was
purchased used from my cousin Brett, who was a used-car dealer
somewhere in Michigan. The only reason my parents made a
non-Ford purchase was that Brett was family and we must have
gotten a really good deal, which is almost as important as being
loyal to a brand if you're from the Midwest. If you're loyal to a
brand, you get a good deal, *and* a family member works for the
company, that is a midwestern trifecta. You'll talk about that for
years to come. The Dodge Charger was two out of three, so we
didn't really mention it much.

My Charger is what I would have described as a burnout car.

It had a hatchback and smelled of old cigarettes, and not mine (I didn't start smoking until months later), so I insisted on burning incense in it. Sometimes I even burned a candle in the cup holder. Not smart, but it improved the stench a bit. My biggest hurdle with my Charger was leaving the lights on. I could never remember to turn those damn lights off. Ever. I started by putting a Post-it note on my steering wheel that said "lights." Well, I got so used to that Post-it being there that I had to add another, and another, and another. Soon there were Post-its all over the interior of my car. My father eventually had to buy me my own jumper cables because I was constantly asking strangers for a jump, and if they didn't have their own cables, I had to wait for the next stranger to walk/drive by. It could end up being hours before I found a willing driver who was packin' his own cables *and* didn't look like he would rape/murder/kidnap me. Those cables were and remain one of the best gifts I've ever received. I got really good at jumping my car and at flagging down random people in the parking lot at Laurel Park Place, the mall where I had my after-school job. I'm certain that just about everyone who worked at that mall gave me a jump start at some point. I always got unnecessarily annoyed at people who weren't willing to help me out—especially considering how deft I'd become at jump-starting my car. I know it probably didn't add up—here I am so stupid that I left my lights on, but smart enough to know how to conduct electricity from one car to another without killing myself or blowing up either car.

Putting those pesky lights aside for a moment, I loved how much crap I could fit in the hatchback of my Charger. One Halloween, my high school boyfriend Eric and I went to pick up my dog from the kennel. There were hundreds of pumpkins on the lawn and the woman in charge told us we could take as many as we wanted for free. I think we took around fifty. We took so many pumpkins that it weighed down the hatch of my car so much that it was almost dragging on the ground. We definitely grounded out when pulling in to and out of parking lots. However, the pumpkins proved to be a great bribe for people skeptical of my battery-jumping ability. Turns out people will let anyone under the hood of their car for a free pumpkin. I probably would. Why not? Eventually, I added an empty gas can to the loot in my hatch for the (many) times when I ran out of gas on the side of the road.

You see, these were pre-cell-phone days, when it was easier to just take care of shit myself than walk all the way to a pay phone, call my dad/mom, and wait for them to come to my rescue, or call AAA and wait for some strange man to come to my rescue. Or worst of all, wait for my mom/dad to call AAA to come to my rescue. I have come to believe, though, that the only modern-day Prince Charming comes in the form of a AAA tow truck driver. Every other Prince Charming is just an impostor who will, no doubt, end up borrowing money from you and eating the leftovers in your fridge you were saving for after work. I guess I'm just a do-it-yourself kind of gal. I'm also way too controlling to be a good damsel in distress.

So, there was only one other little hiccup: I got in the car one morning to go to school, and the driver-side door wouldn't close. The damn thing opened mid-ride! Have you ever driven a car while holding the door shut? It's, like, really hard to do. The door is heavy, especially on a two-door hatchback made in the late 1980s. Turning a corner was torture, and I was extra thankful for my seat belt that day. I had to rethink my usual route in order to turn less. Eventually, I had the door fixed for good, but the fewer-turns route became my usual route, since, as it turns out, fewer turns spilled less wax out of my burning candle. So, you could say my Charger did me well for about a year.

After I left for college, my parents immediately donated the car for the write-off, and I felt a little sad that I didn't get a chance to say good-bye. It was my first material object that offered me independence and seemed to signify my parents' trust in me. My best friend, Nicole, made the two of us these clay figurines for our cars that hung on a rope. I still have mine. I have had him in every car I've ever owned. Sadly, Nicole's is gone because she got carjacked in Detroit after we graduated and it was stolen along with her car. I felt really bad (but not bad enough to offer her mine). Mine has lived in my Escort, my Explorer, both Lincolns, my Audi, and now in my Prius. I call him my hang-in-there guy because he hangs on, no mater what. I think he is good luck. I hesitate to even type this, for jinxing purposes, but I think he is the reason I haven't gotten in a terrible accident, even though I've been told repeatedly that I'm a horrible driver.

So, back to college graduation. As the date neared, my dad asked me what color car I wanted. He told me it would probably be a Ford Escort but wanted to know if I had a color preference. I was getting a free car; I wasn't going to be picky about the color! Bad move. He chose pink. Hot pink. My dad bought me a hot-pink Ford Escort. It shimmered. It was my new car, my graduation present. It is the car I would have to drive until the second I could afford to (a) buy a new one or (b) have it painted a different color. The best/worst part of my new car was that my sweet dad painted a vanity plate for me. In Illinois at the time, you didn't have to have a license plate on the front of your car, so you could put anything you wanted or could fit there, or leave it empty. Well, my father painted me my very own vanity plate that said "★ 2 B" on it. I know, I know, I should have just taken the plate off, but I couldn't do it. Something about taking the front plate off made me feel like I was embarrassed by my dad and how much he loved me. I felt like that plate was my dad in a way, and I didn't want to forget him as I embarked on my postcollege life.

I didn't want him to think for a second that I didn't love all the work he put into it. Just like the lunch bags he drew pictures on for me every day when I was a kid, it was an artistic expression of his love and support, and for an engineer that's a lot. Besides, when you're driving an iridescent fuchsia car around, people don't really notice the license plates.

The miraculous thing was that eventually I sort of forgot

about how embarrassed it all made me. I had my own car, so anyone who made fun could suck it. I think my friends knew if they wanted to borrow it or needed a ride to the airport, they'd better keep their mouths shut about my star—and they did. One day I drove past my friend JP walking in Wicker Park. I honked my horn and waved at him, and he yelled out, "Hey!! It's the Star 2 B!!!!!" I remember being totally embarrassed, but I couldn't stop laughing anyway. For as long as I can remember, my father seemed to be the only person who had faith in my future STARmeter (that's the thing on IMDb.com that tells you how famous you are at that moment. It is horrible and I am sure has driven many people to drink). My father was beyond confident that I would someday be a star . . . of some kind. Did he think, all those years ago, that I would be a movie star? Maybe? Probably. My father has loved me more unselfishly than any other human male I have ever known, and seems to have never-ending faith in my career and abilities, and even though I think the plate should be changed to read "Co ★ 2 B," I know my father would tell you he painted it right the first time.

My dad taught me to drive the day it was legally possible to do so. I was fifteen years old, and in Michigan you could sign up for drivers' ed on your fifteenth birthday. So I did. I took the class, did the driving part, got my permit, and hit the road. It was very important to my dad that I have a lot of driving practice before I went out solo. And I did. My parents were really into road trips, so I drove them all over the Midwest. I drove when we went to visit family in Ohio, I drove to downtown Detroit to Red Wings games, I drove anywhere and everywhere. I learned to drive in our Lincoln Town Car, and to this day that is my dream car. I ride in them often now for work, since they are the go-to car for car services that get hired to drive actors around because we can't be trusted to get places on time. And every time I ride in one, I secretly wish I was driving it. It was a lovely car to drive. It was giant. It was comfortable, like driving around your living room, and trust me, if you can parallel park a Town Car, you can pretty much parallel park anything. Once I moved to L.A. with the ★ 2 B and got some decent-paying acting jobs, I was urged to lease a car for the write-off. I leased a Ford Explorer (still brand loyal) and decided to donate my fuchsia Escort to a charity. I was going to go with the Red Cross, but a friend told me I should choose a charity that could really use the donation, and people donated millions to the Red Cross every year. Why not choose a local charity that was overlooked? I chose a shelter for battered women in downtown Los Angeles. It seemed like a good one, it was local to L.A., was a great cause, and could, no doubt, use the donation. Well, it turned out it did need the donation, but it also needed someone to figure out what to do with that kind of dona-tion, and unfortunately all I had to offer was the car itself. A man came to my apartment to pick up my car and do the paperwork. I gave him all the papers I could find that said "Escort" on them, signed some of his papers, and that was that.

A few months passed, and one afternoon a police officer knocked on my door asking if I was the owner of a hot-pink Ford Escort. I could finally say no to that question! Well, it turned out I was lying to the cop because I was still, legally, the owner of that car. The people at the local charity of my choice hadn't done their part and transferred the title; instead, they left it parked outside somewhere, and it had collected enough unpaid parking tickets that I now had a warrant out for my arrest. It now seems like a miracle that I got that officer to go away that afternoon without me in handcuffs. I explained to him what I had done and pro-duced the documents that showed I had donated the car (another miracle that I still had those papers and could find them). I still believe in donating money and stuff to small local charities that really need it, but maybe make sure there is an infrastructure to support the donation as it comes in. I found out after I followed up that the ★ 2 B was ultimately sold to a junkyard for parts, and it really depressed me. Still does. It makes me sad for two reasons. One, that the car was just basically wasted. My friend JP moved to L.A. later that year, and I could have just given him the car. He didn't have one, and you kind of need a car in L.A. And two, that I was so embarrassed of my car that I felt I needed a new one for my new life. But the truth is that that car *was* my life. It was representative of who I was, where I came from, and how much I was loved by my parents. But I wanted to start over. I was in Hollywood, I was an actress, and I thought I was better than that car. Fifteen years later I finally learned that no one is better, especially me, than a hot-pink Escort and a vanity plate painted with love.

My Stupid Trip (Alone) to Spain

I'VE ALWAYS WANTED TO BE THE KIND OF WOMAN who traveled by herself. I loved reading books about adventurous women who would just travel somewhere, anywhere they were curious about, with or without a travel companion, just because they felt like it. Those women were independent, confident, mysterious, sexy, and interesting. They had great stories to tell, could appreciate art and architecture, had friends all over the world, and the coolest clothes purchased at international flea markets. OK, maybe the last reason was number one on my mental list. If I heard one more girl respond to a compliment on a skirt or jacket with "I got it in a flea market in Paris," I was going to scream. *I* wanted to be the flea-market-in-Paris girl. But the other stuff was important too. I wanted to learn about all the things that I didn't get to in college because I was acting all the time. I had made a promise to myself when I realized what a conservatory was and that I was in one that I would self-educate when I graduated, and what better way to boost my intellect (and wardrobe) than international travel? Instead of just reading about history, why not go see it for myself? I was an only child. I was used to spending time by myself. I had traveled a little already for work, I mean to Phoenix, Casa Grande, and Kenosha, but still, I was adventurous. I moved to L.A. by myself . . . that's something, right? So I decided that if I wanted to be that kind of woman, I should just do it. People traveled alone all the time—so why not me? If you want to do something, just do it, right, Nike? So I did it!

I decided to go to Spain—Barcelona, to be exact, and spend a week and a half there. I didn't know anything about Spain, I didn't speak Spanish, but I chose Barcelona anyway for a few reasons: (1) my friend Martin had gone there alone the summer before and said it was beautiful and safe and everyone was nice and spoke English; (2) I loved the movie *Barcelona* by Whit Stillman; (3) I knew a guy from high school who was living there, so I had a local emergency contact.

The first thing I learned about myself, minutes after deplaning, was that I am not one of those people who should travel by herself. I don't like it. I didn't like walking through the airport. I didn't like trying to get a taxi. I didn't like riding in the taxi to my hotel, and I *really* didn't like it when I got to my hotel. You see, the night before there was a riot in the neighborhood where I was staying, so the streets were deserted and all the storefronts were vandalized. There was spray painting everywhere, not that I could read it, but I'm pretty sure whatever words were spray painted under the Chanel store sign weren't words of social encouragement and positivity. Many windows were broken and boarded up, and there was still glass and garbage littering the streets and sidewalks. I'm not sure if I would have been any better off had things been totally normal, but my trip was off to a rocky start, and I can't say that I ever fully recovered from my immediate conviction that this was a bad idea for me.

The daytime was better. I enjoyed being alone in parks, deciding how much time to spend in museums, where I wanted to go, where and when I wanted to shop, and how late to sleep in. It was all up to me. And I did love that. I figured out how to get around (kind of). But when the sun went down, it sucked. It was dark, I was alone, I was scared, and it seemed to cancel out whatever strides I'd made in my independence during the day. When I was back at my hotel with only my thoughts and the same six Euro MTV videos on a loop to keep me company, I always found myself wondering, why did I do this again?

I was nervous to do pretty much anything at night, even walk around. The city looked different to me when it was dark. I was scared to use a map because I thought I would be a target for possible rapists, thieves, or even a group of rambunctious teenagers. I guess I wasn't the savvy traveler I thought I was because I was always making a wrong turn and winding up on a quiet, empty street. I knew there had to be people out eating, drinking, and having fun, obviously this was happening somewhere, I just couldn't find where, and I felt left out. I used the Internet cafés, sometimes I pretended I was in a Bourne movie and that I was undercover, I would type really loud and fast, eyes clocking all the exits. That was fun for about thirty minutes. I finally e-mailed my friend Martin, the one who had been to Barcelona and had the best time by himself (liar), and was like, "WHAT THE FUCK? What do I do here? You said everyone would want to talk to me. No one does. You said everyone spoke English. No one does. You said I would meet people, I haven't met anyone. I'm sad and lonely and I think I hate you. Why am I so lame?"

The night before had been my breaking point. I'd hid in my room the majority of the evenings so far, only really venturing out to go to a nearby Thai restaurant (pad Thai is still a real comfort food for me). While I was out wandering around (read: getting lost) that day, I passed a cool-looking restaurant. It was tucked into a charming courtyard, and the food people were eating for lunch looked amazing. So that night, I was going to be brave—ready or not. I was going to embrace the woman who, for some reason, thought she'd like to be the kind who traveled by herself. I hailed a taxi at my hotel and told the driver the address. And to my delight, he was excited that I was American! *Finally!* It turns out he had been working on his English and wanted to have a conversation with me. Of course, the first thing he asked me was if I was meeting my husband at dinner. No.

"Fiancé?"

"No."

"Boyfriend?"

"Nope."

"Ah! Girlfriend!"

"*No*, I am going to dinner alone. I'm not meeting anyone."

"'Alone'? What is this word? I don't know this word."

Are you fucking kidding me? "Alone. It means with no one. Just me."

"*Ah!* You have no one?"

Jesus Christ. "Yeah, just me. I have no one to eat dinner with."

"Alone?"

"YES."

"Just you. No one. Alone?"

"YES. Just me."

He handed me a Spanish-English dictionary. "Will you find 'alone'?"

I took it, found "alone" in English. I handed it back to him. He read the meaning in Spanish and started saying the word over and over, "Alone. You are alone. You have no one. Alone. Just you. Alone. Alone. You are alone."

Seriously, I am not making this up. Next, he handed me a small computer and requested that I type the word "alone." He was keeping a list of new words so he could remember them. It was one of those translator devices they sell in the back of the *SkyMall* catalog, so, shaking my head in disbelief, I typed, "ALONE."

He took back the device and read it out loud. "Alone." Finally, just before the pit in my throat worked its way to my tear ducts, I began laughing. And I couldn't stop. He was saying the word over and over and trying to put it in sentences, all of these new sentences about me, naturally, and how alone I was and how I was going to dinner alone. That no one was meeting me, ever. That I would be alone forever. That I would never share a meal with anyone ever again. OK, that was my subtext, but basically this fucking guy said, about fifty times, that I was alone. NO SHIT DUDE! At this point, I was laughing so hard tears were rolling down my face. We finally pulled up to the restaurant, and he turned around, faced me, and said, "I will eat dinner with you tonight so you don't have to eat alone." I had finally made a friend in Spain.

I've heard of several girls with this brand of wanderlust. Is it the early to mid-twenties that inspires it? Finally having a little money of our own? A fear of becoming too settled and never having the chance again? Of not trusting our type A personalities to allow such frivolous pursuits once we got further down our career paths? Or was it just, simply, to see if we could actually do it? For me, I think it was that. I did it. It's not my thing, but now I know. I can still be an adventurous woman, I just want to adventure with someone else, or at least meet someone for dinner afterward. I decided not to accept my taxi driver's offer that night to be my dinner companion. I was sufficiently cheered up and, for the first time all week, looking forward to sitting at the restaurant bar with my phrase book and novel, alone.

How Shopping Changed My Life

THERE ARE A LOT OF DIFFERENT FACTORS THAT CON-tributed to my being an actor. There is my early dancing "career" (not nearly as exciting as it sounds in my bio), joining a theater program in high school, and going to an acting conservatory for college, but the real answer about how I got my big break is this: I was walking down the street in Chicago in a vintage blue rain-coat, and for the second time during my five years living there, I was "discovered."

It was raining and I was just weeks away from graduating from college. I was walking to my restaurant job, and a woman ran across the street and yelled at me to freeze. She asked me if I was a model. I'm not kidding. I told her no through my laughter but that I was just about to graduate from acting school, and did that count? She said my raincoat was fabulous, and I looked fabulous, and she could help me become even more fabulous. Uh, yes please!

It turned out that she was an agent and represented models and actresses, and I just happened to be walking down the same street as her office. I was going to need an agent, so this was really perfect. I got her a stack of my brand-new head shots, and she started sending me on auditions.

My acting program prevented students from auditioning professionally until after graduation; that was a rule. Though apparently *everyone* but me was already breaking that rule. It wasn't like I was such a rule follower, just lazy, and this rule functioned as a perfect excuse. So, once I got my new agent, I got sent on some weird regional commercial auditions, which sucked, and I never booked any of them. I auditioned for some industrial films, which were awesome, but for the wrong reasons. In case you don't know, industrial films are short movies made by companies to demonstrate something to their employees, like training videos. It's stiff competition for those roles. Some of those guys were making almost five figures acting in them, and a new face in the waiting room was threatening, even if I was a twenty-one-year-old girl and didn't own a suit and was never going to get cast as a corporate CEO or regional sales manager. The actors who considered these jobs their bread and butter wore these devices called earwigs. One man I met at an audition told me if I wanted to get serious about industrials, I would need to invest in an earwig. Earwigs look like baby hearing aids that are actually teeny tiny recorders; they're flesh colored and stick in your ear. They are very expensive and could be customized to match your specific skin tone, hair color, whatever you want. You record your lines, and the earwig plays it back for you right in your ear! That way you never have to memorize "the MOR reports are to be categorized by HP22-578 label E4." Who could memorize that? Who would want to?

I digress, but seriously, if it's true that we only use 10 percent of our brain space, do I really want to use some of it up on that kind of stuff? The answer is yes because there was no way in hell

I was spending my bartending dollars on an earwig. My bartending dollars were being spent on ridiculously tight pleather pants that could be hosed off at the end of a shift and would help me earn more dollars; *that* was money well spent. Anyway, after my first few industrial film auditions, I knew I wouldn't be booking any of those, nor did I really want to. Maybe if there had been a good one, like a sexual harassment orientation video or security breach protocol movie in the style of a Jason Bourne film, those would have been the ones to fight for, but no such luck. But who cares, I had the main thing I needed most after graduation, an agent!

The second time my raincoat worked its magic was at my first movie audition. It was for *Kissing a Fool*, starring David Schwimmer, Jason Leigh, and Mili Avital. It was shooting over the summer in Chicago, and they wanted to cast a local actor in the role of Mili's visiting cousin. It was raining on the day of my audition, so, of course, I wore my blue raincoat and decided to use it as a prop during my scene for the casting director. In the audition scene I was getting ready to go out and Mili's character was asking where I was going, so I put the coat on while answering her question. My raincoat clearly made an impression because when the director came to town for callbacks, he asked for me. I auditioned for him, and when I was finished, he didn't say anything about my performance but asked where the raincoat I used in my tape was. It was sunny and hot on the day of my callback, so I said, "Look out the window, it's not raining, so I didn't wear it."

I don't know if it was my sassy comeback or the memory of that raincoat from my tape, but I got the part! Of course, not without promising him and the two producers that I would wear the raincoat in the movie. I shot *Kissing a Fool* the summer after I graduated from acting school. I got another movie after that, a guest spot on a TV show that shot in Chicago, and then a play.

I was a working actor starting the day I graduated. It's not the best story to tell actors who are just starting out. I feel guilty that I had such a smooth beginning in Chicago. And how do I tell people who ask me what they should do to get an agent? Should I lend them my raincoat? I even ended up getting another agent soon after my raincoat discovery. My first agent decided after she signed me to leave the business and pursue her dream of becoming Jodie Foster's character Clarice Starling from *The Silence of the Lambs* and joined the FBI. My new and improved agent only had a few clients, and he treated us like we were his children. He was direct and honest. He never let us wallow if we didn't get a part, but would somehow manage to build us up for next time. His name was Chuck Saucier, and he was the one who really started to carve out a career for me, not just get me auditions.

The magical blue raincoat still hangs in my closet. No matter how many closet purges I do, I could never get rid of it. I haven't worn it in years, but every now and then I get it out and try it on. I recently bought myself a new jacket. It's a black leather motorcycle jacket. I've always wanted one and finally decided it was time. I doubt people will ever stop me on the street because of it, but when I wear it, it makes me feel the same way my old blue coat did—really cool. I sometimes wonder if it was the jacket that attracted the attention or the way I felt when I was wearing it. And could my "big break" really be because of a raincoat? The years of ballet, high school plays and musicals, four years and thousands and thousands of dollars for acting school, was it even necessary? Or did it boil down to one day of thrift shopping in Chicago? Guess it doesn't really matter because here I am, but if it *was* the shopping, I have a good argument for how to spend my next day off.

Home Is Where the Cops Shine Their Helicopter Lights

EVEN THOUGH I KNEW I HAD TO COME TO LOS ANGELES to pursue my chosen career, I was afraid to move here. I had probably watched too many hair-band music videos as a kid, but I didn't want to be that girl getting off a bus on the corner of Hollywood and Vine with a suitcase and a dream, only to find herself, years later, in a music video wearing a lace teddy and writhing on a hot rod for drug money while still telling her parents she was "acting." L.A. scared me, and I quickly decided I wasn't going to stick around to see what happened if I didn't get acting work. I was going to give myself a little time, I am somewhat patient, but I didn't want to live here forever, still don't. It is a huge city, spread out and connected by roads that are covered in cars that all slam on their brakes the minute I get behind them. Trying to drive here is like standing in line for a one-stall bathroom at a nightclub, but with sixteen feet of car wrapped around you. The weather in L.A. is almost perfect every day, yet no one ever seems to be outside. No one walks anywhere. People drive everywhere, and mostly with the windows up. Maybe because of the smoggy air, or maybe they're ashamed of what they are listening to during their commute. Before I moved here from the Midwest, I thought everyone here would have a convertible, but they don't. And I get it. When I see one now, I assume it's a tourist. I rented one once when I came for a visit, but my advice is, save your money. You will get a weird sunburn, and everyone will be staring at you assuming you are a tourist. It's rare to drive above thirty-five miles per hour here, so that dream of the wind blowing your hair around while you speed up the Pacific Coast Highway watching the sunset over the ocean will probably be just that, a dream. Spend the extra money on drinks at a beachfront bar instead. Trust me.

Before I committed to L.A. and got an apartment, I was homeless, but not like *real* homeless. I was starting-out-actor homeless. It's the kind of homeless where you have a bunch of crap in your car but haul it into whichever apartment you are crashing in at the moment. When I booked my first few jobs in Hollywood, I was sleeping on the carpeted floor of an empty bedroom in my friend Sean Gunn's apartment in Westwood. His roommate hadn't arrived yet, so I had the room until he did. I slept on a pile of blankets because I was too cheap to spring for an air mattress. At an audition one day the casting directors asked about my move and my plans to become local. I told them I wasn't going back to Chicago for a while but needed to find an apartment because I didn't want to share a bathroom anymore with a boy if I wasn't at least sleeping with him too, and Sean and I were not that brand of friends. They told me to drive up Beachwood Canyon in the Hollywood area and check out the bulletin board outside the Beachwood Market: there were always lists of apartments that were available, and they were usually more eccentric than the lists the rental companies had. I was secretly pleased that they thought I was the type of person who would enjoy an "eccentric" apartment. Now I know that term was probably code for cheap and weird. I had never seen anything like Beachwood Canyon before. It was so charming, and as I drove up that hill and saw the old buildings and bungalows, I knew I wanted to live there. If you're not familiar with L.A., it is the canyon directly under the Hollywood sign. It's literally the Hollywood Hills. When I looked at the bulletin board, I was heartbroken to find there were no apartments available in Beachwood Canyon proper, but there was an ad for one in the Beachwood Canyon area. (By the way, this is a total real estate lie. When they say "area" or "adjacent," they are lying.) The little one-bedroom was in Hollywood, *not* Beachwood Canyon "area" as promised, a few blocks from the intersection of Hollywood and Western. My first clue that this was not the neighborhood of my Hollywood dreams was the constant sound of helicopters flying overhead, and at night that sound was accompanied by these bright helicopter lights that shone directly into my living room. My apartment was on the first floor, front unit. All that separated my living room from the criminals being chased outside were four ancient French doors with locks similar to those in a bathroom stall. I am shocked and thrilled that during the few years I lived there, I never got robbed. I wish someone would have told me, "Don't live where there are cops driving around all the time." I blame it on my midwestern naïveté, but I thought that made the place safer. Nope! If cops are around all the time, that is because there is a *need* for cops to be around all the time.

There was also no parking lot/garage for my building, and there was no street parking to be found ever, at all, never, at any time. There was chatter about some extra spaces that you could rent in the lot of the building a few doors down, and I did ask to be on the wait list for a spot should one become available—

but it never happened. I had to park blocks and blocks away. Parking blocks away to the west wasn't as unsafe as blocks away to the east. West was medium, east was bad. I kept weird hours because I was always coming home late from work, or if I wasn't working, I was coming home late from hanging out with Sean. Most nights I ended up walking several blocks home alone pretending I was Linda Hamilton from *The Terminator* so I seemed tough and un-rapeable.

The building itself was cute. It was old and charming, probably from the 1920s. Every building in L.A. seems like it was built in either the 1920s, the 1950s, or the 1980s, never before, in between, or after those decades. My building had a lot more character than the other buildings on my street (which resembled a run-down set of *Miami Vice*, the series, not the movie), and there was always a healthy amount of sofas on the curb if you felt like lounging with the tracksuited Armenian men who populated "Beachwood Canyon area," a.k.a. Little Armenia. These men hung out on the curb all day long and into the night. I assumed they were actors too, since they never went anywhere or did anything. I guess they could have been writers. It always confounds me how few people in L.A. seem to have a job to go to. Doesn't *anyone* work in this town? I find myself yelling this out loud in my car when there's bumper-to-bumper traffic at 11:00 a.m. on a weekday. Perhaps everyone here is a delivery person of some sort—I still really can't figure it out.

With all my stuff still in a storage space in Chicago, I pieced together some furniture to make my new apartment a home. I scored a mattress off a production assistant from an independent movie I was shooting when he moved in with his girlfriend and didn't need it anymore. I got an armchair off the same movie. The producers asked me to work overtime for free, which is fine, but their mistake was asking me inside the vintage furniture store we had been shooting in. I told them that if they bought me the green chair I had been eyeing all day, I'd do it. It was forty dollars. I worked hours and hours of overtime on that film, no one ever saw the movie, but I still have that chair. I bought a white TV/VCR combo, covered the box it came in with a scarf, and sat the TV on top. Finally, I found some nesting tables and a lamp at a local vintage shop, and I was set. I was happy there. Eventually, I had my stuff shipped out from Chicago, but when it came, I didn't unpack the boxes for the longest time. I liked living with no stuff, probably due to my mom's obsessive-compulsive spring/summer/fall/winter clean outs, but whatever the reason it kept my new life very simple. I also thought it would be easier for the potential robbers if they could just carry out boxes instead of having to tear the place apart to find my valuables. Less mess for me.

I tried to make some friends in my building—that didn't go well. First, there was the gay couple that "watched" my apartment when I would travel. We had a miscommunication. To me, "watch" meant make sure no one steals my shit. To them, "watch" meant steal my shit. I should have figured it out when they told me that they fixed the drawer pulls on my dresser; I would have just thought I'd lent out all my CDs, books, and jewelry. The guy who had the apartment next door clearly had a cockroach problem because he would constantly bomb, which only forced the bugs to run into my apartment. There should be a label on the cockroach-killer bottle that reads, "If you live in an apartment building, be sure to warn your neighbors you're bombing, as the cockroaches will probably just run next door. They're not as stupid as you are filthy." I actually went on a few dates with the guy across the hall. He was cute, but I remembered my mom always telling me not to shit where I ate, and that seemed like what I was doing if I dated a guy in my building. Also, he had lost the hearing in one of his ears, which he said threw off his balance, and therefore could only stand if there was something he could hang on to or he would lose his balance and fall right over. Perhaps you think me shallow, but at that time in my life I just wasn't ready for that kind of caregiving in a relationship. He did take me out for Indian food on our first date. I'd never had Indian food before, and I have loved it ever since. My plan was to stay in the building until something great opened up in the actual canyon. I checked the bulletin board several times, but I tend toward laziness. Luckily I met an actress who had a great little place up there and said I could take over the lease when she moved in with her boyfriend. I felt my apartment hunting was done and I could wait it out while eating Slim Jims and drinking Diet Coke with the Armenians on the street sofas. What I didn't anticipate was how long it was going to take her to actually move in with her boyfriend. It took a *really* long time. Like, over a year. But eventually she did, and I finally got to move to actual Beachwood Canyon.

The upgraded apartment was in a house that had been divided into three separate units. It was a little more expensive but totally worth it. It had a huge bedroom, a little living room, a tiny kitchen, weirdly, two full bathrooms, and quarter laundry in the building next door I was allowed to use. I called it my tree house and I loved it. But what I loved most didn't have anything to do with the apartment; it was that I finally had a parking space to call my own. In the driveway. Right in front of my door. That only I was allowed to park in. This was major. I was right around the corner from a charming café and an overpriced market and right under the Hollywood sign. If the wind was right, I could probably have hit it with a well-constructed paper airplane.

Ironically, the location, what I longed for most of all, turned out to be the only problem with my new apartment—and it was a life-and-death one. Literally. When I was waiting to find my tree house, it never occurred to me that the Hollywood sign was a major tourist destination, that the only street I could take to get home thousands of people would drive their cars halfway up, pull over, and run into the middle of to photograph the sign. Huge tour buses of elderly people, foreign tourists, children, all jumping out of these buses, cars, vans, and walking purposefully, not looking both ways, into the middle of the main artery for this neighborhood, to take a shitty photograph of the Hollywood sign. Or, better yet, to have someone else photograph them under the sign pretending they're holding it up! But what I really came to resent were the looks of apology that people would feign as they darted out in front of my car. One day, after I almost killed an elderly Asian tourist, I vowed to go to every bookstore I ever passed for the rest of my life and rip out the chapter in all the tour books that tells you to stand in the middle of that street for a great shot of the Hollywood sign. Tour book writers: STOP FUCKING WRITING THAT! YOU'RE GOING TO GET YOUR READERS KILLED! I did a spit take one day when I found out that there was talk of lighting the Hollywood sign. The community was really against it for historical reasons. I was against it because when it was dark out, and the most dangerous time for potentially hitting a tourist, there were no tourists since the sign was not visible at night. Thank *God*. I had just about as much as I could handle during the day. People, if you find yourself going to L.A. anytime soon, please just buy a postcard photo of the sign. I am not saying to not drive up there and see it, sure, do that. Get a coffee at the café, or even better, go horseback riding at Sunset Ranch and take a million photos of it from the trail on your horsey ride, but please, I beg you, do not exit your vehicle and stand directly in the middle of a road and take a picture. If you ignore this warning, I promise you will hear obscenities being screamed at you from the swerving cars.

However, none of these screaming people will be me. No, I

have since moved on. I now have a less interactive view of the sign. I can still see it from my front yard, but I no longer fear committing homicide every time I drive home. When I was finally looking to buy a place, I saw so many different houses in so many different neighborhoods. I wanted to get away from the "sign." I wanted to get away from the helicopters, cockroaches, and thieves. But in the end, like the crime family to Michael Corleone, it pulled me back in. My house was the only one I could find that I could afford. Call me superstitious, but maybe since I had made it this far staring at those famous white letters every day, I shouldn't leave it behind just yet. I wonder if that iconic sign was somehow watching out for me as much as I was forced to watch out for its fans, and I realized I just wasn't ready to leave "Hollywood" for good.

I think it was once I bought my house that I really felt at home in Los Angeles. Moving to L.A. is really hard. I had an easy time getting work, but fitting in and making friends was another story. I wanted a home, but I didn't have a lot of faith in Hollywood. I didn't want to get hurt and have an awkward breakup with it. I wanted it to be a clean split if it happened. And to me, a clean split meant not settling in. But time passed, and not settling in started to mean I wasn't committing completely to my work and my life here, and I was ready to commit. Besides, at a certain point I had no other skills and nowhere else to go. When I told people I couldn't get another job besides acting, that I wasn't qualified for anything else, they'd often say, "Oh, please, if you can use Excel, you can get a job." This proves my point because I didn't (and don't) know how to use Excel. I had no friends left in Chicago or Detroit, and I couldn't use this famous Excel people spoke so highly of, so I reluctantly found myself at home in L.A.

When I look back at my first five years in Los Angeles, I don't think it was the places I lived and their unique disabilities that kept me from feeling at home—I think it was that fear. I was afraid of failing. I was afraid this town would eat me up, but while I was fighting it and not paying attention, I was planting roots. Time goes by fast in Southern California. I blame the weather. It's pretty much always warm and sunny, and the seasons are so mild you blink and it's been five years, blink again and it's ten. It's hard to track time here, because it doesn't change much. Leaves stay green and they stay put, and by accident I did too.

Part 2

Hollywood Life

Judy Greer Is My Name. Well, Now It Is.

WHEN I LANDED MY FIRST PROFESSIONAL ACTING job and had to join SAG, the actors' union, my given name was Judy Evans. My full legal name is and always has been Judith Therese Evans. For some reason, the Internet Movie Database (IMDb) insists my middle name is Laura—but it is wrong and, it turns out, impossible to bargain with. At the time I joined the union, you could only have one name per member, and there was already a Judi Evans; she was on my awesome babysitter Shirley's soap, *Days of Our Lives*, which made it my soap, too. Judi Evans played Adrienne Kiriakis, a real pillar of the *Days* community, and in the early days of my career (and life) I didn't feel comfortable using our shared name. She had it first and she was really good. I had a decision to make. I could be Judith Therese Evans, Judith T. Evans, Judy Therese Evans, Judy T. Evans, or, as my mom's side of the family called me to avoid confusion with my aunt, Baby Judy. And even though, legally, all of those options except Baby Judy could get me on an airplane using my driver's license, all those names felt like someone else's.

Having three names felt too fancy, and I am not fancy. Being called Judith just made me feel bad about myself because the only time I ever heard it was when I was in trouble and my dad went full name on me, or when the kids in school yelled "Judas Priest!" in the halls when I walked by. I had a long talk (approximately eight minutes) with my parents about changing my name from Judy Evans, and we decided I should stay Judy but change the Evans to a different family name.

My dad's mom's last name was very Serbian and hard to spell and pronounce. So that was out. I still have no idea how to spell it. However, my mom's grandmother's last name was McGuire. Judy McGuire had a cute ring to it. The fact that I was drinking Guinness in Irish pubs all over Chicago at the time might have had a little something to do with my decision as well. On the night I settled on my new name, I fell asleep (passed out) happy with my new identity and excited about the future of Judy McGuire. The next afternoon, I arose from my drunken slumber to find a giant billboard right outside my window of Tom Cruise, laughing in his sunglasses, with two giant words next to his giant face: Jerry Maguire. In fact, the entire city of Chicago was painted with posters and billboards of it. I felt like I was in a *Punk'd* episode—everywhere I went, there was my almost-new name, sides of buses, benches, posters plastered all over construction site walls, phone poles. Maybe they did this for every movie, but with this one I felt bombarded; it seemed like overkill.

Now, remember, this was before the Internet. I didn't know Tom Cruise was starring in a movie called *Jerry Maguire* seconds after he was cast in it. To add to the equation, I was finishing college, so even if there was Internet, I totally had my head up my own ass and probably wouldn't have used it anyway (someone recently told me there was Internet back then and a computer lab on campus too. Huh?). If you didn't go to school with me or live in the apartment complex I spied on across the street, I didn't pay attention to you. After I saw that famous grin looking at me through my bedroom window, I felt at a loss. I didn't want to be Judy McGuire anymore. I wanted something new, something different. I knew that the Jerry Maguire movement would have to eventually die down, but I didn't want to wait that long. I wanted my name to be new and exciting now; I wanted to be ahead of the curve! The only option, as I could see it in that moment, was to steal the identity of Big Judy, my aunt Judy Greer. She was the Big to my Baby. She was the woman I was named after. It immediately made so much sense that I was mad at myself for not thinking of it sooner.

My parents claimed that they knew several Judys and liked them all, so that's why they chose that name. But, to me, Big Judy was the best, so I give her full credit for my first name. (Also, my dad dated a Judy before my mom, and I've always thought it was a little weird Judy was even a potential name for me in the first place but whatever, I guess my mom isn't as needy and competitive as I am.) Judy Greer married her high school sweetheart, Jerry Hershman, and became Judy Hershman. But since she never moved from the town she grew up in, people knew her as both. Perhaps Judy Greer felt right because I had heard it my whole life, or maybe because I loved my aunt Judy so much and she was so special. Either way, I just knew it was the one, so that's the name I finally decided on when I joined SAG.

By the way, if you're reading this and you have any pull with the people at IMDb.com, could you do me a favor and tell them that there is not, nor has ever been, a Laura in my name? I don't know how they got that information, but they are wrong. And I am prepared to show my birth certificate if that's what it takes. It makes no sense: if I'm going to lie about anything at this point, it's going to be my age, not my name.

It Takes a Village

M. NIGHT SHYAMALAN WAS THE FIRST DIRECTOR TO call me on the phone himself to offer me a role in his movie. The movie was called *The Village*. I auditioned on tape in L.A. and then flew to New York to meet him in person for the final call-back. The next day he called my cell phone and asked me if he could send me the script and if I would play the role I auditioned for. I was in a taxicab when I got his call, and when I hung up, my driver was the first person I told; he didn't understand what I was telling him, but I could tell he sensed it was good news and that if he acted excited, his tip would reflect that. I had just finished shooting *13 Going on 30* and was so excited to have another great project so soon after. M. Night Shyamalan directed huge-budget movies, and I was going to be in one! (Take that, everyone who made fun of me in high school!)

It was my first big role in a big-budget film that shot outside L.A. I'd been in some big movies before, but either they weren't on location, or my roles were so small I was only there for a few days, and in both cases I was too nervous to pay attention to anything but not screwing up. I had yet to experience anything like *The Village*. I would be working on the same movie for three months and living in the middle of the woods in Bucks County, Pennsylvania. My career was getting real.

One of the many things that made an impression on me from that movie was the size of the crew and how appreciative Night was of them—at least that's how it seemed to me. He insisted that we were fed well, he hired the same people over and over again (meaning the crew; he hasn't hired me since), and every Friday at lunch the names of all the crew members were put in a pot, someone would draw a name, and that person would win a trip for two to some fabulous destination—I remember Hawaii and London being two of the places. The actors weren't eligible for Night's trips, only the crew, and that's when it occurred to me that they are the ones who really make a movie happen.

I couldn't get over how many different jobs there were on a set! There are guys who have to put plywood boards all over base camp because when it rained there would be mud everywhere and we might slip and fall and break something important. There was the costume department, which had to tie us into our corsets every morning, untie us at lunch, tie us back in after lunch, and then out again at the end of the day. Our hair and makeup artists, who had to plaster our hair down to our skulls, put our wigs on, and then take them off at the end of the day, clean and prep them for the next day of work, and unplaster our hair. The camera department has to haul all the lights and camera equipment out of the trucks every day and load them back in every night. Sometimes hundreds of people are responsible for a movie. The actors, writers, director, cinematographers, designers, and producers are so outnumbered that I always wonder, if a director is being a total asshole, why isn't there a coup?

I don't know how many people were on the crew of *The Village*, but I just finished shooting *Dawn of the Planet of the Apes*, and I asked someone on set how many people were working on the movie. It seemed like for every one person on set, there were two somewhere else in the world working on it as well, in offices, doing special effects, etc. At one point thirteen hundred people were employed by *DOTPOTA*! (That's what we called it due to the title length and verbal laziness.) That's a lot of cast and crew on set, a lot of personalities spending fifteen-plus hours a day together, for several months, far away from all their homes and families. And in the case of *DOTPOTA* the weather was either cold and rainy every day in Vancouver or stiflingly hot and humid in New Orleans. There were guys on that movie who were paid to light stuff on fire and guys paid to make sure that the other stuff didn't burn. There were trucks that were delivered by even bigger trucks, and different people to drive them both. At the bar after work you could have drinks with an actor, helicopter pilot, truck driver, and makeup artist, all working on the same job! It's a small town of people all working together to make something that only exists at that moment in the minds of a few people. Yes, everyone is getting paid for their work, but still, I think it's impressive. This really makes me realize the beauty of the movie and TV industry, and even though I've been doing it for years, I never tire of it. Well, except for one thing. I get really bummed when I'm in a movie with someone amazing and I don't even get to meet that person. I'm thinking specifically of Meryl Streep. I mean, come on . . . it's MERYL!!!

Another movie I did called *Jeff, Who Lives at Home* was a much smaller film. The crew was about forty to fifty people, but they were no less impressive to me on set. There was no budget for lobster and steak at lunch, like some of the giant sets I've been on (although we did have a crawfish boil one night after work, which was awesome because I got to hold a baby alligator), and people were doing several jobs at once, but I could really feel how excited everyone was to be working on our little movie. And

Jay and Mark Duplass, our co-directors, knew everyone's name and always smiled and said good morning and thank you. They were great bosses, and I could tell they were genuinely grateful to everyone who came to work every day ready to work hard, have fun, and help them tell their story. One thing I appreciate about the crew is that, like the mailman/woman, they are there every day. Rain, shine, freezing cold, sweltering heat, 5:00 a.m. call times, no matter what. They don't get to call in sick. They don't get to take breaks in trailers like we actors do. They are the village that it takes to make a movie—no job is too big, no job is too small, and all of them are the filmmakers.

The Week I
Had a Beard

MY MANAGER CALLED ME ONE DAY AND ASKED IF I wanted to play a bearded lady for a week on the television show *My Name Is Earl*. Naturally, like any forward-thinking woman of the twenty-first century, I wanted to do this. I mean, how many times in a lifetime does a lady get to wear a full beard? Well, except for actual bearded ladies. Those women would probably jump at the chance to play a role that *didn't* have a beard (note to self: don't take non-bearded roles for granted anymore). Anyway, I was excited. It would be a fun new challenge! And that's what I'm always trying to do with my career.

The show brought in a special makeup artist just for me and my beard. She was lovely and awesome and I forget her name because I'm the worst, but we got really close that week. It's personal work to apply a beard, and it took her a few hours to do it. She created four beard pieces that were glued on my face, and following that she would add individual hairs to connect the pieces. While she did it, I couldn't move or talk or eat. It even took a while to remove my beard at the end of each day. She had to be really careful not to ruin the four original pieces and not to burn my face off with remover chemicals in the process. Some of my face burned off anyway, which I don't blame her for, it's just an occupational hazard. And at least it wasn't razor burn. In theory this all sounded really cool, but in reality it was one of the weirdest weeks of my life.

Having a full beard made me feel really sad. Mostly because, with all that hair glued to my face, I couldn't smile! So, for an entire week of work, I had to try not to see/hear/think of anything that made me laugh or smile. It was also very hard to talk or eat with my beard on. I couldn't open my mouth that wide, so sandwiches were out, and anything drippy like pasta or soup was majorly problematic because it would get all over my beard and that was super gross. And the truth is I love a breakfast burrito— it's one of the treats I allow myself when I'm working on a short job—but that was not even close to an option. I couldn't scream. I couldn't yawn. And I didn't recognize myself in the mirror at all. I had longish hair at the time, and if I parted it down the middle and wore aviator sunglasses, I looked exactly like Chris Robinson from the Black Crowes. It was kind of mesmerizing, but for the most part it was sad. I would just sit and stare at myself. It was like I was staring at another person. I felt like I was in an eighties movie where people swapped bodies, but my movie swap was way more indie, on account of the fact that I couldn't make any wacky faces during the discovery process or injure myself trying to swap back. I just stared at myself while sipping hot tea through a straw that was melting. Very indie indeed.

Because the character I was playing was the bearded lady in a circus of human freaks, the props department made a poster of me for set decoration. It was pretty big, four feet by two feet-ish. When the episode wrapped, props gave me the sign to keep. I put it in the trunk of my car, facing up, and forgot about it until my car got searched when driving on the CBS lot several weeks later. The security guard gave me a really weird look after checking my trunk for explosives or kidnapped celebrities, but I had totally forgotten that the sign was still in it. It wasn't until I got groceries later that day and popped my trunk that I saw my bearded face staring back at me. And seeing my solemn expression brought back all those melancholy bearded emotions. I felt bad for my bearded self, that she never got the chance to find happiness with her beard, that she never figured out how to smile. Which is why, if there's a next time, I'm going to insist she can smile, even if it adds two hours to the beard-laying process. I feel she deserves at least that.

Press Junkets

A PRESS JUNKET IS A WEEKEND-LONG EVENT WHERE the main people involved in a film sit in a fancy hotel room and members of the press come in one at a time, for two minutes each, and ask you about the project you're there to promote. But here's the weird thing: I can't tell them anything juicy or potentially damaging about the people involved or the production. I would lose my acting license, and no one would ever hire me again. OK, there's no such thing as an acting license, and I'm not famous enough for my interviews to damage my career. But I'm no tattletale, although maybe sharing some dirt could potentially work to my advantage . . . Nah, it's not worth it. Besides, I don't really have any dirt. When you're a co-star, you're not really around long enough to get any good dirt. Basically, at a press junket, I'm there to sit in a chair, look pretty, and say that all the actors were great, that the director was great, that making the movie was fun/important/life changing/great, talk about why I wanted the role (so I can pay my bills), and tell a moving story about shooting or a practical joke that someone played on set. This last question gets asked a lot when you work with a known practical joker like George Clooney. So, why do we do junkets if everyone is just going to say everything was great? To get people excited about the movie! And it is exciting. It takes about a year from the time you shoot the movie for it to be ready to be released in the theaters. So it's been a year since I've seen the other actors, the director, and the producer. And I get to go to a screening of the film so I know what I'm talking about (and if I was edited out). After that first screening I always wonder if it's going to be a huge hit. Will it change the way people view movies forever? Will everyone be a better person after seeing it? Will America be a better place once this movie is released? Usually, in my experience, the answer to all those questions is not really, but talking about it for two days before the release does get everyone all fired up, just in case.

Sometimes after sitting in the same dark room, answering the same questions over and over, I start to go a little nuts. Isn't that a definition of insanity? Doing the same thing over and over expecting a different outcome? I think I read that somewhere, probably a self-help book. Anyway, a few years ago a publicist taught me how to make it fun. I play the junket game! And I am totally victorious at this game. Between each interview, someone from my crew gives me a new word to fit into my answer, any word, and I have to naturally and honestly incorporate it into my answers during that two-minute interview.

I really excelled at this during the junket for *Elizabethtown*. My standout was "alligator." When asked how I liked working with Susan Sarandon, I remember saying to one journalist that Susan Sarandon and I got along so well we were like two alligators swimming in the Everglades. Alligators in the Everglades? Do they even swim in pairs? I got a full three seconds of silence from my interviewer. That is the one I'm most proud of. It was awesome—and the crew gets a kick out of the game too. "Helicopter" was a really hard one, especially since I don't do action movies, but I did it. I bet you a movie ticket that I can work any word into an interview without lying. Susan and I did get along like two alligators. And Jennifer Aniston is as sweet as a lollipop. Katherine Heigl does not ossify dialogue—she brings it to life! So, while you don't often see my interviews, because I am just a co-star, if you happen to catch one, see if you can pick out my word. I bet you can't . . .

FAQ

recognizable but not immediately able to place. It happens to me every day of my life if I leave the house—someone wants to know how they know me, what I was in, who I am, and generally why I look so familiar. There has to be an answer, and they need to know it right away. I am not complaining. I knew this was a possibility when I started working more and more. And in a lot of ways it's the best of all worlds. I can go about my business, run errands, get drinks at a bar, floss my teeth in a public restroom, read a book in a park, walk my dog in my jammies, and maybe I have to answer one of these questions, but I still have my privacy. Every once in a while a weird thing happens, though, that is uncomfortable for everyone involved. It's when neither the fan nor I can figure out what they know me from. It starts out innocently enough: A person is so enthusiastic about getting my identity right and they are excited to meet me, even though they don't really know why yet. I am feeling flattered and I want to help. The question in these scenarios is usually, "Aren't you an actress? I know you! What are you in?" I begin with fan profiling (see my introduction if you skipped it), but when my first few tries fail, I have to go to phase two and ask what they like, TV, movies, romantic comedies, indies? The answer will usually be either "Everything" or "I don't watch TV, and I never go to the movies." Now the fan is getting a little impatient, and I start to sweat. My fan starts to doubt me, thinks I'm trying to pull one over on them. But wait, he/she stopped *me*! My fan will try to help: "Well, what's the last thing you were in?" "Um . . . [enter last project here]?" I squirm. The fan says with a sigh, "No. I didn't see that." I will then list a few other credits. "No. No. Maybe. No." I make a last-ditch effort, I'm feeling like shit, the fan is irritated, we're both late, I blurt out something obscure like, *"The TV Set?"* Fan says, deadpan, "Yeah. That's it. Cool. Well, 'bye. Nice to meet you." Fan has lied. We both know this is a lie, but we're both relieved because we both want this interaction to end, we need it to end. I need it to end because I have been forced to list every job I've had in the last fifteen years in order to prove something to a total stranger and I have failed, and Fan wants it to end because now I'm not as shiny and exciting anymore. Fan feels duped, and I'm probably not even the person he/she thought I was in the first place. Fan won't remember me anyway, and I will just re-promise myself I will never engage like that again. Sometimes I get fun questions like if I'm in a punk rock band. Sometimes I get drunk-girl questions like, "You're . . . OHMYGOD! You're her! Are you her?" I try to be nice. I try to answer them with a smile on my face even if I'm holding my bleeding arm in an ER in the middle of the night. Here are a few of the questions most people who walk by me in an airport, shopping mall, restaurant, bar, ER, Starbucks, bathroom, funeral (I could go on here, but you get it), tend to ask. I've included my answers since maybe you're wondering too. In fact, you may have been one of the people to ask me.

Q: What do I know you from?
A: First of all, hi. Second of all, that's a tough one. I can't read your mind, and I don't know what you've watched

recently. Maybe if I hung out with you for a short while, I could make a proper assessment of your tastes and give you an idea. Or you could just ask my name and Google me later. There's also IMDb, do you know that Web site? I think you'd like it. It's pretty easy to use, and it will answer all your questions. I've been in about forty movies and who knows how many television shows. It would take me a really long time to list them all for you, but, hey, if you have the time, let's do this! I'm sure I can just catch the next plane to my destination. Yeah, I'm running through an airport, but whatever, let's figure this out together.

Q: What are you in?

A: Clothes. A building, just like you! My skin? See answer above.

Q: Is *Arrested Development* coming back?

A: I don't know, and if I did, why would I tell you before it was officially announced? (Before Netflix released the new episodes, I got asked this question all the time. Now that Netflix has shown all the newest episodes, I thought my days answering this question were over. And I was right, they are. What I didn't think about was the new question.)

Q: Will there be an *Arrested Development* movie?

A: I don't know, and if I did, why would I tell you before it was officially announced? No one tells me anything. But if I find out there is, well, I probably still won't tell you, because I wouldn't be allowed to talk about it. So I guess you'll find out when it's officially announced, and a little bit after I do.

Q: Have you ever done stand-up?

A: No, I don't have what it takes to do that. I can hardly handle a snippy parking lot attendant, not to mention a roomful of people expecting me to make them laugh. I think my heart would stop on that stage or I would become a raging alcoholic. Or both.

Q: Did you do Second City?

A: Nope, even though I am mainly in comedies and went to college in Chicago, I didn't. I've never even seen a performance at Second City. I'd worry I'm not funny enough, and Second City seems really intense and cutthroat. I would burst into tears, and then no one would take me seriously. I'd be the crying girl and get kicked out during my first week of PMS. However, I do now realize the error of my ways. There are so many cool people I could have met, and I think it would have made me funnier and tougher, assuming I could cry in private, but again, I would have no doubt ended up a raging alcoholic.

Q: What's Charlie Sheen like?

A: Really? Still? What do you think he's like? He was nice to me but put a lit cigarette out in my fresh cup of coffee, and for that I will always hold a grudge. It took a long time to finally get to enjoy that cup of coffee, and I had made it just right. It *is* the little things sometimes, you know?

Q: How come you haven't starred in a movie yet?

A: Well, it doesn't really work like that. I don't know, it's not like there's an audition form with star and co-star boxes and I keep accidentally checking the co-star box. Maybe I'm not good/funny/pretty enough? I really don't know. I'm trying, don't you worry, but believe it or not, it's not *that* easy to get to star in a movie. But I promise you (and myself) I will keep trying. But for now, please know that I am very happy with my career. I work all the time, and I can still go to Target without a security team. What more could I ask for? OK, you know what I mean. But, if you're so inclined, feel free to start a campaign on my behalf.

Q: Are you a cop?

A: Whaaaa? Me? A cop? I mean, that's awesome, but no way.
(I am not making this up. It has been one of my favorites.
A lot of people recognize me but don't know why. Once
I got pulled over for not coming to a complete stop at a
four-way intersection, and when the cop walked up to
my window and took a good look at me, he asked me that
question. I burst out laughing.)

Q: Do you live at the Lake of the Ozarks?

A: Uh . . . no.

Q: I love *Bridesmaids*! Can I get a photo?

A: Sure! You know I'm not in it, right?

Q: Aren't you that actress?

A: Yes. I am.

Celebrities I've Peed Next To

THERE ARE A LOT OF PERKS WHEN YOU'RE AN ACTOR. Free food at work was my second favorite in the beginning, but my first, I have to admit, was the weird stuff. Like seeing celebrities at 5:00 a.m. in no makeup, finding out what they ate and what size shoes they wore, and admittedly the weirdest was listening to them pee. It didn't happen often, and I don't have a fetish or anything, maybe I shouldn't even call it a perk, but there is something so humanizing about bodily functions. I think it's what really levels the playing field. I have peed next to several *very* A-list celebrities, and every time I hear the tinkle of celebrity pee, I giggle. I have no idea why. They have to pee—I know that—but you know how when you were a kid, it was really jarring to see your teachers outside school, or walking to their car, or crying? That's what it's like. In fact, that's how I feel about celebrities doing anything normal—not "stars, they're just like us" normal stuff, but *really* normal stuff, like peeing, getting blood drawn, having cramps, dropping their house keys seven times when walking from their car to their front door, forgetting to change out of their slippers before leaving the house for the day, having a really ratty bathrobe that they never, ever wash, etc., etc. Another aspect of celebrity life that I also envision is that they are so busy and have no free time ever. That they must always be at a fabulous party or rushing from an airport to a photo shoot and then to a fabulous party while sending hundreds of e-mails/texts/tweets from two different smart phones. I imagine that their homes are meticulously organized, that their dogs don't fight, that they have never had a squirrel die inside the walls of their house which attracted every fly in Southern California, that they have great hair all the time, and that their washing machines don't break down mid-load the night before a trip.

But what I also wonder—as I stress out about missing a recording session for *Archer*, the animated show I do a voice on for FX, or figure out when I'm flying up to Oakland for a recording session at Pixar, or panic about how I'm going to find time to write this book, while I shoot a video for my Web series, *Reluctantly Healthy*, pack for a month in New Orleans, get another job, read all the scripts that have been e-mailed to me—is if maybe I *am* busier than a real celebrity. I can't afford a full-time assistant to organize my life, I don't have a chef cooking meals for me and my family, I barely have time to work out or walk my dog (OK, fine, I do a have a dog walker. I mean, I'm not going to shortchange my dog Buckley, come on). And don't even get me started on trying to see my friends and still have a social life with my husband and stepkids. It's a lot to keep straight!

Whenever I begin this rant to my friends, though, I think of *Runner's World*. Have you heard of that magazine? I used to have a subscription back when I ran (or had time to run), and I was always inspired by the articles it printed about the people training for races. Sometimes it was for a marathon, sometimes just a 5K, but no matter what, these men and women not only inspired me but reminded me to shut up and stop complaining. I read an article once about a single mother of five (did you catch that? SINGLE MOTHER OF FIVE!) who worked full-time and trained for and ran a marathon!! What the . . . ??!! How did she do that? How did she manage to still feed her offspring? And work? And sleep? And do laundry? And run? She must have a superpower. I think there should be a section of those rag mags called "normal people, they're better than us!" Because trust me, it's not as hard to get to work on time if someone is picking you up and driving you there.

Another celebrity lifestyle question I always had was, how did they travel? I knew they did, because there are photos of their bikini-clad bodies everywhere, and I assume they all don't fly on private jets, it's so bad for the environment, and since they all drive Priuses, I know they care. Well, either way, I was right. Traveling is different for celebrities and civilian mega-rich people. Did you know there are people you can hire at airports called greeters? I don't know how much they cost (I'm sure it's not cheap), but they have been provided for me a few times in the past. Their whole job is to meet your car when you get dropped off! Before you ever reach the greeter, a town car is hired to pick you up and drive you to or from the airport. Well, most of the time. Sometimes (or maybe it's just me) you're driven by a PA, or production assistant. I was once driven from the airport to my hotel by a PA in a pickup truck covered in dog hair and slobber. On that day I realized why professional drivers get hired. I didn't say anything to production, though. I have dogs and didn't care that much, but I cannot imagine someone like Sir Ben Kingsley having his suitcase thrown in the cab of that truck and having to make small talk about the particular breed of herding dog whose fleece was everywhere and the constant sinus infections the dog is plagued with in the winter months (turns out it wasn't all slobber). Anyway, the airport greeter gets your boarding passes for you, walks you through security, gets you settled in the lounge, then, when it's time to board, walks you to your gate. If you have one of these people, you literally can be sleepwalking through the airport and still get on your flight (I have seen this happen). I had never heard of this magical greeter person until a studio hired one for me. I felt so fancy! The only problem is it's just like flying first class for work: you get used to it, and then it sucks when you're back in coach and crammed next to the one person who packed a tuna salad sandwich. Sigh . . . Is it better to have loved and lost than never to have loved at all? I think yes, especially if you get free drinks during the love.

Celebrities are also really great at charity. I didn't even realize how great until I experienced it firsthand. At the table read for the movie *The Wedding Planner*, I valeted my car at the hotel where we had the read. When it was over, I realized I didn't have enough cash in my wallet (it cost almost the same as my rent to valet my car at this hotel), and when I went to the ATM to take out money, I had insufficient funds and couldn't get any! I panicked. How would I get my car? Should I walk home? Walk to a friend's house and borrow some money and walk back? Just give up altogether and move back to Chicago? Apparently, I had been cursing at my stupidity out loud because I heard a voice behind me say, "Need to borrow some cash?" Humiliation complete. It was Matthew McConaughey and his longtime friend/driver. They insisted on giving me cash to get my car out. I was mortified but also relieved because my friend Sean was my emergency contact, and he wasn't picking up his phone. I was good for it and paid him back on my first day of work. Well, I gave the money to his driver—I was too embarrassed to hand it to Matthew in the hair and makeup trailer in front of everybody.

Of all the celebrities I've peed next to, I'd say I was most nervous peeing next to J.Lo. Heidi Klum didn't make me nervous, because I didn't realize it was her until we came out of our stalls at the same time. Debra Messing made me a little nervous, but mostly because the bathroom was really quiet and I was feeling a little gassy that day. Many of the other tandem pees were with celebrities I was working with, so there was usually a lot of talking over the pee and I wasn't so focused on it. On one indie movie I did, we were all sharing trailers, so everyone used the Andy Gump portable toilets to avoid any weirdness, sounds, odors, and so on. But I remember peeing next to Jennifer Lopez really well. This was a long time ago, she wasn't even J.Lo yet, and it's not her pee I remember, but being next to her in a stall on a soundstage while shooting *The Wedding Planner* and thinking to myself, "I can't believe I'm peeing next to Jennifer Lopez!!!! This is so cool!!!" We went into the bathroom together, well, at the same time, and I wondered while I squatted if she would wait for me when she was done and take that moment to confess that she was hoping we could become real-life best friends, not just movie best friends. With no one around to listen in, she may have even wanted to tell me a secret or ask me about my beauty routine! She didn't. She was gone when I came out of my stall. Why should she wait, though? We weren't friends or anything. I would have waited for her, but only because I feel that in life, if you go to the bathroom with a girl, you should wait for her before leaving unless otherwise agreed upon. Isn't that girl code? Or am I wrong about that? I guess in most cases girls who go to the ladies' room together don't have bodyguards waiting outside the door, so that does change things slightly. Or does it? What's the girl code for going to the loo in pairs if one of the pairs has a bodyguard and is super famous and they aren't really friends, just co-workers?

Speaking of bodyguards . . . They are cool. And badass. And weird. I have never gotten used to being next to someone who I know has a gun on them, at least not until I married my husband and had to sit next to his ex-wife at the kids' Little League and soccer games. She's a sheriff, and if she's not in uniform, she always has a gun in her purse, because, well, you never know, or so she says. I wonder why the celebrity bodyguards carry them, though. And I wonder if these celebrities I'm peeing next to have stalkers. And if they do, am I in danger too? And if I am in danger, is it worse that J.Lo left me alone to fend for myself post-urination or better? Was she actually protecting me by distancing herself from me physically? (Maybe she does want to be best friends after all! And I am just making this connection now! Oh, J.Lo, did I let you down? *Crap!*) More likely, she could tell how naturally tough and intimidating I am and that I would be able to fend for myself if things got physical. I'm not from "the" block, but I lived on a block, in a subdivision—that counts, right? Oh, and I have some advice for all you stalkers out there . . . Stalk someone who doesn't have a giant bodyguard trained in Native American martial arts Israeli warfare boxing and is carrying a *gun*. Really, are you *that* crazy?

The Ultimate
Best Friend

IN MY EXPERT OPINION (AND I DO THINK I CAN CALL myself an absolute expert here), the ultimate movie best friend was Kit from *Pretty Woman*. People weren't that familiar with Laura San Giacomo before that movie came out, but she was funny, cute, sassy, and approachable. She stole our hearts and achieved the ultimate romantic comedy goal of helping us fall head over heels in love with Julia Roberts. Of course Julia would have an amazing best friend who would be so fun and funny, and of course Julia would give her best friend a rolled-up wad of cash so she could get off the streets (or go to the not-free clinic). I mean, duh. That movie made everyone want to become best friends with a hooker, or become one so Richard Gere could sweep them off their feet.

Here's my theory: movie studios know that the star of the movie is someone no one can really identify with because we know too much about her—she's too beautiful, she's too rich— but once you give that gorgeous A-lister a blue-collar bestie, she suddenly becomes more relatable. Because the real secret is that best friend is you! If that actress (what's her name again?) can be best friends with Julia Roberts/Jennifer Aniston/Cameron Diaz/Jennifer Garner, then so can *you*! Yes, we all want to be the star, we want to be the girl who gets the guy in the end, but the more realistic scenario is that we could maybe, actually be that person's best friend. Movie stars have to have best friends too, don't they? That special someone who will show up with ice cream in the middle of the night, who will slap some sense into them when they are being whiny, who will drop everything to meet them in the ladies' room of the restaurant where they are on their first date with Paul Rudd to coach them through the lie they told to get asked out in the first place.

I do have a question for moviemakers, though. How come it seems like girls in romantic comedies only have one friend? And how come it's always someone they work with? I know it's easier to condense work and best friend scenes, but really? Everyone just happens to be best friends with their co-workers? If a movie was made about *my* best friend and the filmmakers just made her partner at work her bestie, I'd be pissed. My best friend didn't call that co-worker to meet her at Starbucks in the middle of the day when she dropped her son off on the first day of preschool! That co-worker didn't spend the night in the hospital waiting room during my best friend's C-section! That co-worker didn't drive to Vegas so my best friend wouldn't be alone on my best friend's thirtieth birthday! Did my co-worker plan my entire wedding, even though she was going through a terrible divorce? NO! Maybe it's because what our leading lady is doing is so stupid, and something she's done a million times before, that her *real* best friends don't have time for that shit anymore, so she has to rely on fresh co-worker ears for a little sympathy before she makes the real phone calls, the phone calls that are going to hurt because that real best friend is the person who will tell her that she's being an idiot again. And because she knows she will have to give back the jeans she borrowed, and she's not ready to give them up just yet.

I think there needs to be more real best friend movies. I loved *Bridesmaids*. I believed that Kristen Wiig and Maya Rudolph were actual best friends. It was a platonic comedy about an actual friendship. It's a girl-gets-girl movie (but not in a lesbian way). I also loved how the other bridesmaids fulfilled different roles in the life of Annie (Kristen Wiig's character). I have a few really close friends. If anyone made a movie about me chasing the boy I ultimately ended up with forever, there would be so many different conversations and phone calls with all my best friends, because it's just not realistic to have only one. You need different things from different people, and I feel like, with my gals (and one guy), I have all the bases covered. I would call Kelly for her fiery no-questions-asked support, Sean for an impartial male opinion, Sarah for a sympathetic ear, Lola for a completely different take on situations and general fabulousness, and Janet for all of the above. Oh, and with the exception of Sean, I can borrow clothes from all of them—that's key. They like each other but aren't really friends outside me. There would never be a scene in the Judy Greer movie where we all got together to discuss the dumb thing I just did. I wish that would happen, but real life doesn't really work like that. Plus, we're all really busy, some have kids, crazy jobs, Sarah lives in New Jersey, and sometimes you just can't meet at a moment's notice at a centrally located sports bar in a fabulous outfit (wait, I'm thinking TV best friends; movie best friends meet in chic mixology lounges).

One thing I have learned from playing sidekick characters is to be direct and honest. There isn't a lot of time in an hour and a half to beat around the bush, you don't want to get edited out, and you're responsible for a lot of exposition. For example, many of my lines go like this:

- "You know you do this all the time. Remember Rick last summer?"
- "But you lost all that weight after Bob dumped you!"
- "There isn't any time if we have to be at the important thing by eight!"
- "Not *him*! HIM."
- "This reminds me of when you shit your pants climbing out of Ted Vadella's window in seventh grade." (This is a good one because I'm establishing that she's a pants-shitter and it foreshadows a possible flare-up later in the film.)

And so the writing for these BFFs is short and sweet, with jokes peppered in.

But what does it take to be a real-life best friend? I get asked "What kind of friend are you in real life?" a lot. I always just make something up, but this seemed like a perfect opportunity to find out what my friends had to say about my personal best friend-ness. First, I'd like to say that it took a while to get the answers back. Because, you see, my friends are busy, so they couldn't just drop everything and write loving e-mails to me about how awesome I am. Some had to be pushed. One still hasn't responded (Lola!), but here's the roundup, in order of response, because that seemed the most fair. And I'm fucking fair, damn it. It begins with my e-mail to them.

Dear friends,

A small favor? I am writing a chapter in my book that I think is going to be about being a best friend in the movies and about being a best friend in real life and was wondering, if you had a few minutes, if you could write a few sentences about what I am like as a friend in real life. You don't have to, and I don't even know if I'll use them, but you can say whatever you want, and I promise you won't hurt my feelings because I am fairly confident that you all love me a lot.

Thanks,
Judy

P.S. You will get no money or writing credit for this, a martini or glass of wine, maybe.

SARAH. FIRST TO RESPOND. I HAD TO INCLUDE THE BEGINNING BIT BECAUSE I LIKE REAL LIFE THE MOST.

hi lady.

sorry it's taken me a while to get back to you. end of the school year crap is making me crazy!!! and then they captured a bear in our town this morning but before that happened they had to cancel field day and it's just made the schedule today all crazy.

anyway, you know what i think of you as a real life best friend? i think you're awesome. and i think it's awesome that we can go for a month without talking (not that i like that) and it feels like i just talked to you yesterday. and even when we're both busy, i know you'd be there for me if i really really needed you. i love that you are honest all the time, and that you some-times push me to be more honest with myself. i like that we can both be really silly sometimes about stupid shit, like our visionary lipstick, or blind cleaning ladies. i like that we can talk about how good it feels to take a great dump. i like that we both appreciate and understand our needs for expensive shoes and handbags. overall, i think we're a pretty good match. if you were cast in a movie as my best friend, there would be a lot of sequels, because i don't ever want to stop being best friends. i don't have anything mean or critical to say, because i do love you and i think you're great.

hope the writing is going well. sorry i was late to the game on this.

xo, sarah [SHE WAS THE FIRST ONE!]

SEAN—FIRST E-MAIL EXCHANGE

On Jun 13, 2013, at 7:03 PM, Judy wrote:

did you send the thing for my book? i feel like I saw an e-mail from you, but i can't find it now. if not, no worries . . . might be losing my mind.

glad you're good and happy. miss you though.

On Jun 13, 2013, at 11:37 AM, Sean Gunn wrote:

I didn't yet, but I will definitely do it before I go to bed tonight (so, before 5pm your time).

Sent from my iPad

On Jun 14, 2013, at 1:14 PM, Judy wrote:

(in a whiny voice with british accent) oh i'm sean and i'm in london and i'm in a different time zone than you . . . wa wa wa . . .

On Jun 14, 2013, at 1:26 PM, Sean Gunn wrote:

Fine, then here's mine: "I've known Judy for 20 years and she's always been a total fucking bitch. Like, ALWAYS."

Sent from my iPad

SEAN—FOLLOW UP E-MAIL

Judy and I have been friends for 20 years, and the thing that makes her so easy to be with is the true joy she finds in all aspects of life. If I want to be silly, she'll joke around with gusto, if I want to be intellectual she'll talk with gusto about any topic, and if I need a sympathetic ear she'll patiently listen to my problems and give me the best advice I can get. It's really that simple. This passion is also what makes her such a superb actress. Oh, and another important thing to know is that she loves giving money and other gifts to strangers. Don't believe me? Just walk up to her and ask!

KELLY

Trying to lay out in words, what it's like being best friends with Judy is tricky yet terribly simple.

There is an unconditional love like a sister, so honesty comes easily.

Honesty from Judy comes a bit TOO easily. She is forthright and a ball buster. She wants you to be the best you can be and will hold you to it. She will call you out on your BS. With that said, she's a pretty great listener—so be careful what is thrown out there.

She will laugh hysterically at the most odd moments and stories and sightings. Not caring if anyone else finds it funny, she will laugh to tears (quite often and it's fun to watch!).

Being best friends with Judy always lends itself to "out of the ordinary" outings (going to the Golden Globes, hanging out with George Clooney and friends, movie premieres, etc.) but then will be as humdrum and typical (if not slightly boring) as hanging out with her stepkids and (amazingly awesome) husband at their home in the suburbs.

It's never a dull moment, even when it is dull . . .

It's pretty darn easy and fulfilling, even when it's challenging. Kinda what most all relationships should be like . . .

Xo

JANET

Dear Judy,

You asked me to write a little something about being friends with you. I've been procrastinating, trying to think of the perfect little something to sum it all up, and basically I've boiled it down to this.

You know how we wanted to be John Cusack's girlfriend because we saw what a great boyfriend he was in Say Anything? Or how we're convinced the world is wrong and Gwyneth Paltrow would be so much fun to be friends with? How we constantly romanticize the characters and celebs and assume that who they are on screen, or in magazines, translates to real life?

Well, I am the best friend of the girl who always plays the best friend—the girl in the movies that probably tons of girls think, "I'd totally be friends with her." I am best friends with Hollywood's go-to best friend.

But here's the thing, you're fucking better than all those snarky, quippy, perfectly-made-up-to-look-not-as-pretty-as-you-really-are characters. The real, unscripted you is a thousand times more interesting than any character you've ever played.

The real, unscripted you doesn't always have the perfect comeback. You don't always have good advice (remember when you told me to wear headphones to block out my baby's cry-ing?). You cry fifty-five times a day. You quit too easily. You love Subway. You don't wash your hair enough. You frequently make people uncomfortable by walking around your house naked. You feel sorry for yourself, like, all the fucking time. And your car smells like dog.

You have your shit together but, girl, you are a disaster. And I love it.

I couldn't be friends with Red Carpet you. Because Red Carpet you is just someone else's version of you. I'll take the real thing any day.

Crying now. Fuck.

Love to you my best-est best friend. Don't start getting too good at life—or we'll have a problem.

XOXO,
Janet

(AND THEN THERE WAS THIS TOO)

On Fri, Jun 14, 2013, at 11:44 AM, Judy wrote:

Now I'm crying for a 5th time today. 3 times in spinning this am, once in Old Navy. Why do you have to be so awesome? It makes me miss you more. Next week? Let's get together and get emo-tional.

Oh, and these were really cute at Old Navy. Have them both now. http://oldnavy.gap.com/browse/product.do?cid=26193&vid

=1&pid=385340002 in the lightest color. http://oldnavy.gap.com/browse/product.do?cid=26193&vid=1&pid=387492012

I got a 4 and it's a little big, but your boobs are bigger so it would probably fit you. I'm going to have mine taken in because it was so cheap and so cute.

in tears,
judy

On Fri, Jun 14, 2013, 11:52:52 AM PDT, Janet wrote:

And the last, best reason I'm friends with you . . .
You just said my boobs are bigger than yours.

LOLA

OK, Lola hasn't sent one in yet, because she's being fabulous with her fabulous husband in Mexico, so I will write hers for her. In my fantasy, it would go something like this:

Judy is everything to me. More important to me than my husband, my children, my stepchild, even my parents. In fact, the only thing I love more than Judy is . . . never mind. There is nothing.

OK, fine, I'm taking a lot of poetic license here, but Lola has a way of turning even the simplest activities into something special, and for that I excuse her tardiness.

I did have a moment where I wasn't going to print these e-mails and just save them so I could always read about how much my friends love me and tell them that I played the best joke on them by making them send me these e-mails. That would have been awesome. It especially would have been funny if there wasn't even a best friend chapter in my book and I waited until it came out to tell them about my scheming. Janet was right, I do quit too easily. I'm gonna work on that one, but I will never, and I mean *never*, stop walking around the house naked.

Your Compliments Are Hurting My Feelings

IT'S HARD TO BE AN ACTRESS FOR SEVERAL REASONS, but one is that it's really hard to be constantly scrutinized for things that are not under your control. For example, the way I look. Well, I guess I could get plastic surgery, but that feels cowardly. I have been told that I have a terrible voice. That I'm not pretty enough. That I look tired. That I look unhealthy. That I seem sad (that is mainly a comment I get from people on the street, even before I was an actress). That I have gained weight. That I am too skinny. That my nose is big. I guess if you are willing to put yourself out there, you have to be willing to deal with the consequences. But telling me I am much prettier in person, and why do they make me look so ugly in movies, is not really a compliment. You could stop after "you look so pretty in person." I don't need to know that you think I am ugly in my movies. That doesn't make me feel good or want to take a photo with you. I once got stopped at a Super Bowl party by a girl who was gushing about how she just "couldn't believe" that I was attractive because they made me look so ugly at work, and she wouldn't drop it. She wanted to know how they did it and why I let them do it. You would think these answers were obvious, but I felt compelled to say, "Uh . . . it's not up to me? This is just how I look?" And, by the way, in the movies she was talking about, I actually liked the way I looked.

I also had a real hard time doing press for a film called *Barry Munday*. In that movie I played Ginger Farley, who didn't care how she looked. She didn't bother to do her hair or makeup, she didn't bother to buy flattering clothes or put together cute outfits. When I was doing press for this movie, I was floored at how the reporters reacted to my look in the film. I didn't really do hair and makeup. The makeup artist just put on some tinted moisturizer, a few extra freckles, and cherry ChapStick. I washed my hair and let it air dry. I wore big glasses, and that was about it. All the questions they asked me were about the process to get me looking *so* ugly. "How many hours were you in hair and makeup to achieve that look? Did they use prosthetics? Was it a wig?" I mean, they might as well have been asking me if the creature creators from George Lucas's compound were flown in for our eighteen days of shooting in order to help my transformation along. I mean, really? One couldn't look at me and tell straightaway that the look of Ginger isn't that far off from how I actually look? And, yes, maybe I should be flattered and take it as a compliment that I look so much better in person, but I don't want to translate a person's well wishes. I just want that person to say a nice thing to me or not say anything at all. Remember that saying? Remember learning it in kindergarten?

I know I'm probably extra sensitive, but there are a lot of stupid things that people say. Like, was that your real voice? Did you gain weight for that role? What's your name? I can never remember it. Are you somebody? Why don't you ever want to look pretty in a movie? Do you just not want to be the lead? Isn't it weird that *you* are the one who gets to kiss (George Clooney, Ashton Kutcher, Gerard Butler, Jake Gyllenhaal)?

It's hard to know what to say when you come across an actor you love from movies and television shows, I know, I've had it happen to me. You're not prepared for a chance meeting with someone you recognize but don't know her name or anything she's been in. Well, here is a handy list of possible things to say to a recognizable person:

I like your work.
You are good at what you do.
It's nice to see you in person.
It is so cool to bump into you.
I hope you have a great day.
Keep doing what you're doing, I like it.
You're great. Remind me of your name again?
What can I look forward to watching you in next?
Great work.

Memorize these phrases if you're not cool on your feet (I am not, so I would never judge you) and it will help. One time an employee at Sephora slipped me a note—I still have it. It was sweet and said encouraging words about me being an inspiration to actors. That was nice. He didn't draw attention to me. He didn't ask me my name or what I was in, just kept it low-key and paid me a nice compliment. For all I know he didn't know my name or my work, but wanted to say something nice and planned on figuring it out later.

"I like that you don't try hard" is not something you should say to a stranger. A statement makeover might sound like this:

"You seem mellow and cool about your career." Also, please don't ask me why I wasn't in *Bridesmaids*. It's not for lack of trying, I promise. I auditioned for that movie, like loads of other actresses, but I didn't get the part. It's like asking why I wasn't at the most awesome party of the year so I can tell you I wasn't invited. I will tell you that, believe it or not, I am glad I am not in that movie because if I was, I probably wouldn't enjoy it as much as I do and watch it as often as I do. Although the residuals . . . No, I'm sticking with my answer.

Now, if you know what you know me from, and are excited about it, I'll take that enthusiasm! Yell, clap your hands, squeal with delight, I love it! Tell me you love that movie and why. Show me your boobs and say, "Say good-bye to these!" I love to hear that I'm funny, wouldn't you? I love that you like my work. I do want to know what movie or TV show I've been in that was your favorite. I'll even take a "my cousin has a crush on you," but unless you're getting paid to interview me, please don't ask me why I let them make me look ugly, because maybe I didn't.

Bad Oscar!

IN 2012, I WAS INVITED TO THE OSCARS BECAUSE THE movie I was in for thirteen minutes, *The Descendants*, was nominated. As it turns out, I don't kill it at the Oscars. So many embarrassing things happened in the course of an hour I almost don't know where to start.

Actually, I definitely know where to start: my dress. It was lent to me by the designer Monique Lhuillier, and it was pretty amazing. It was tight, black, and altered to fit my every curve, and there are a lot. It had a thick stripe of silver beads down the front. Tiny little silver beads. Those fucking beads started it all. My very first step on the red carpet, someone stepped on the hem of my dress and the beads just started unraveling. Everywhere. I'd like to take a moment to tell you what a red carpet at the Oscars is like, in case you don't know. Imagine standing in front of bleachers on a high school football field. Now imagine the bleachers are full of people wearing black. Imagine they are all aggressively screaming your name and "Over here! Up here! In the front! To the right! To the left! Move out of the way! [Your name here]!!" as loud as they can. Now add to that image their cameras all flashing together. That's close, but not as intense. The noise is deafening, and the flashes are blinding. Back to me . . . So there are now a hundred little silver beads on the carpet surrounding my dress, and Jessica Chastain is on the carpet behind me. She was nominated, so people were already screaming out her name. I was starting to get trampled due to the fact that I couldn't move because my publicist was on all fours in front of me trying to sew my dress back together and stop any more beads from falling all over the place with the tiny sewing kit she kept in her purse for red-carpet emergencies. It was really hard to hold myself together; I couldn't believe it was happening. I am not cool; I wanted to cry. It was my first Oscars, possibly my only Oscars, and my dress was falling apart right in front of my eyes, right in front of everyone's

eyes, and there was a woman on all fours in front of me as celebrity after celebrity walked past, looking beautiful and confident, wearing dresses that were able to stay in one piece for the twenty-foot walk from car to red carpet. My publicist told me that you couldn't tell, but you totally could. I can tell when I look at the photos. Instead of one thick silver stripe, there are several. I stopped for photos but couldn't do any interviews. I was afraid if I opened my mouth to speak, I would cry, because I was *sobbing* on the inside.

But I survived, as I knew I would, and I walked inside hoping to put it all behind me and have a great time. Commence the next terrible moment. Have you ever gone to a party alone? Have you ever worked up enough courage to go somewhere where you knew you wouldn't know anyone but the host, only to realize upon walking into said party that you'd made a horrible mistake, and you immediately get a drink and stand alone at a cocktail table for what seems like an hour and no one talks to you or even smiles your way? In fact, you are so alone that you want to talk to the guy passing champagne or consider causing him to spill just so you will have something to occupy yourself with for a few minutes. Well, that's phase two of my Oscar experience. I was deposited, by the publicist, at a lonely cocktail table upstairs and told to "have fun," even though I'm still trying not to cry. Really? Have fun? I'm standing by myself at the be-all and end-all of parties. And I know *no one*. There were celebrities all over the red carpet, but where did they go? Where is the rest of my cast? I have been in over forty fucking movies, shouldn't I be at least one degree from everyone here? Where is fucking anyone who looks familiar to me??!!! I grabbed two glasses of champagne hoping to make it look like someone was coming back to the table but planning to drink them both. Thank sweet Jesus and Steve Jobs for the iPhone. I started texting Janet, my best friend.

I generally try not to rely on technology to get me through low-self-esteem moments, but I was desperate. She asked me what Tina Fey would do, and I said that Tina Fey would leave. (This was later confirmed by a director who works with Tina Fey a lot. I felt validated.) Janet felt that Tina would have another glass of champagne (that would have been my fourth) and try to make the best of it. I tweeted too: "At the Oscars!! Holy Shit!!!! (Still standing by myself drinking, like most parties I go to, but, hey, it's the Oscars!)" That made me feel a little better. I was really trying to be positive, even though my dress had fallen apart and I was drinking alone. Still, I was at the *Oscars* wearing a dress that was falling apart and drinking alone, right? A while later I saw my friend Arianne Phillips (nominated that night for costume design for *W.E.*) walking toward me with her boyfriend and parents. I

Selfie at seat-filler bar

was so happy to see a familiar face I almost cried. And, of course, the first thing that Ari said was, "Don't you love coming up to the seat-filler bar? It's so amazing up here." It suddenly made sense. I was in the wrong bar. That's why I didn't recognize anyone. Great. I asked Arianne where people I would know were drinking, and she told me, "Downstairs. Downstairs is the main bar. Everybody's downstairs." Well, glass half-full (er, more like four empty), at least I was buzzed and I got to see Ari.

Terrible moment number three: I decided it was time to go to the bathroom to throw out my Spanx. Yes, I know that is wasteful, but I have to tell you in case you don't wear Spanx, they fucking suck, and if you do wear them, then you totally know what I mean. However, they are a necessary evil; *everyone* wears them. My friend Natalya said once, at an event, "If everyone in this room right now took off their clothes, no one would be naked." She's right. They are so uncomfortable that I wear them for the red carpet only—it's a little deal I made with myself—and if I ever get to carry a handbag that is larger than my fist, I will roll them in a small ball, save them, and not be so wasteful. But until that day, I toss them in the garbage after photos are taken and hope that they get rescued and worn by a woman who, like me, has some dimples on the other two cheeks she'd like to hide. Once in my stall, I started to pull my dress up from the bottom, only to realize that it wouldn't fit over my hips. The dress had been too well tailored, and I couldn't pull it up at all.

This was the moment I realized that for the entire evening every time I have to go to the bathroom, I have to take off my dress, completely. This is the reason I don't like jumpsuits or one-piece bathing suits. It's not that I have a fear of being naked. I have a fear of being naked in a bathroom at the moment we get "the big one," and I get mortally crushed by the building falling in on me. And weeks later, when a rescue team uncovers my body,

I will be naked, and the story (if there is one . . . there better be one) in the news will be "recognizable actress whose name we can't place is found naked in the rubble that was once the bathroom of the Kodak Theatre." I mean, would anyone understand that I *had* to take off my dress completely in order to pee? Perhaps the seamstress who tailored it for me would. But could she be trusted to spread the word after my death? Doubtful.

Beads were still falling on tile, but I didn't care anymore. Photos were over, my Spanx were in the garbage, and I was moments from sitting in my seat and watching the Oscars! I finally got really excited. I mean, what else could go wrong? I shall tell you, terrible moment number four: I was ushered in with my cast (I finally found them in the correct bar). And, of course, I had to walk past the front row and all the biggest and skinniest celebri-

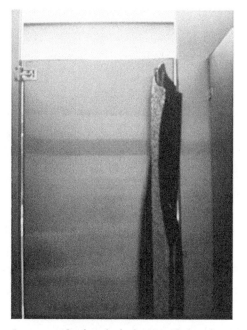

I was completely naked when I took this photo.

ties of the moment. I pass George Clooney, who is the star of the movie I was there for, Brad, Angie, Meryl—they're all there and I'm there too and it was really starting to hit me how so supercool this is, when I saw my friend Suzan about five rows back waving at me, with a shadow of concern starting to appear in her eyes. I waved and went back to chatting up Stacy Keibler, when I saw Suzan again holding up her cell phone and pointing to it. Uh-oh. I hurry to my seat and get out my phone to read, "Your lingerie straps are hanging out of your dress." Of course they are! You have got to be fucking kidding me forever. Can I die? Can I just have a do over? After everything else, I have this? Was I feeling sorry for myself? Yeah, probably. But come *on*! Beads falling off, drinking solo for a half hour, having to strip down completely to pee, and now my straps were hanging out? In front of Meryl?!

LESSONS LEARNED:

1. Sample dresses are potentially poorly made and need to be handled as such.
2. Have a bathroom strategy in place for the evening.
3. Load a book on my iPhone so I can at least read something interesting while I stand alone at parties from now on.
4. CUT OFF LINGERIE STRAPS FROM MY GARMENT BEFORE WEARING!
5. Don't forget to have fun!

You may be wondering what I did with the dress, did I at least get to keep it? Nope. Months later, I got a box with a scented candle and one of those jars of oil with sticks in it. That was my thank you. I know it's not the designer's fault, but still, I'd like to put the woman who actually made that dress on a red carpet, surround her with celebrities, and slowly unravel the beads on her dress, while three tiers of photographers snap her picture and scream her name at the top of their lungs. I should just wear Puma from now on. I've run marathons in their stuff and it holds up just fine. Way to go, Puma!

I sound bitter. I don't want to be the kind of girl who lets one silly little thing (or four) ruin her big night. And ultimately it didn't. I got to go to the Oscars and the Governors Ball, then I got to I meet up with my Prince Charming and take him with me to the *Vanity Fair* party, we ate and drank for free all night (not including fourth meal at the Taco Bell drive-thru), I met loads of people (who will never remember meeting me), and I held an Oscar statue (not mine)! I mean, jeez, Cinderella went to a ball all by herself, had a crazy-early curfew, and lost a shoe, but she still managed to have the best time of her life. At least I didn't lose my shoe!

Papa, Paparazzi

I DON'T USUALLY GET MY PHOTO TAKEN BY PAPARAZZI, but if I do, I assume all the other celebrities are in foreign lands at film festivals I wasn't invited to or that the shutterbugs are mistaking me for someone else, Kathy Griffin perhaps. Last fall I did my first Broadway play starring Norbert Leo Butz and Katie Holmes (she's so cool, by the way, in case you were wondering). Needless to say, there were always loads of paparazzi waiting outside the stage door to get a shot of Katie as she walked from her car door to the door of the theater—it's about a ten-foot distance, who knows what could happen in that ten feet. In the beginning of rehearsal and previews, I tried to dress cute every day, just in case they got a shot of me behind Katie, or if they happened to be whipping their cameras around to catch Al Pacino getting out of his town car across the street at the theater where he was working. Who knows, there might be a flash of my navy beret or a glimpse of my leopard-print jeans I bought in a shopping spree at Target. After a few weeks I ran out of cute outfits and realized it didn't matter anyway, so I stopped trying so hard to look cute as I walked to the theater. Don't get me wrong, I still wore my navy beret à la Mary Richards from *The Mary Tyler*

Moore Show because I *was* going to make it after all and some sunglasses because I did my makeup once I was backstage, and without makeup on I look slightly anemic and like I've been crying for a while (I am not anemic and probably hadn't been crying for *that* long; that's just the no-makeup look I was blessed with). I'd hate to get stuck behind Katie with no makeup on and no sunglasses while they were snapping away at her. If those photos were sold to a magazine, it would probably be for a story about how Katie Holmes was donating her time to a fancy charity and taking a clinically depressed, anemic woman to work with her for the day (again, not depressed and not anemic).

A few weeks prior, my husband (Dean Johnsen) had borrowed a guitar from Norbert Leo Butz (two-time Tony Award winner just in case you're not familiar with his awesomeness) in order to learn a song to perform at the Johnsen family talent show that Christmas. Norbert needed the guitar back so *he* could learn a song for an actual New Year's Eve show he was performing in, for money. Since Dean Johnsen was just trying to impress his siblings and wasn't actually furthering his career or earning money to feed his family or pay his mortgage, his guitar time was quickly up, and I had to lug the thing back to work that evening. My husband asked if I felt comfortable carrying the guitar to work and if I thought that the photographers waiting outside the stage door for Katie would get a photo of me carrying a guitar. "Wouldn't that be funny?" he said. No. As it turns out, my husband is smarter than I gave him credit for, and just as he predicted, the second I approached the stage door, the paparazzi, who *never* take my photo, started taking my photo. The worst part was that they were yelling, "Judy, can we get one with your guitar? Can you hold your guitar up?!" The horror. They asked me to lift "my" guitar higher so it could be in the shot. I would just like to say, for the record, I do *not* play the guitar. I do not own a guitar. I am in no way a musician, I can't sing, I am musically challenged. I took piano lessons for six years, once a week, and cannot play a note. I was just carrying the guitar as a favor for my husband.

For me, the few times I've been papped, it's like running into an ex: it only happens when I look like shit, have pinkeye, or post-yoga crotch sweat. Every fucking time. I could walk to Starbucks seven times a day looking like a normal human American girl, but the one day I am dressed like an extra from *The Hunger Games*, I get snapped.

I clearly have not come very far with my emotional development, because just as I am completely outraged at the photographers' presence, I am later equally hurt when the photos are never printed. My brain is saying I want to be left alone, but my delicate actor ego is wondering why they don't care about me? The photos must be worth so little my mom would probably pay more for a current picture of me than any magazine. She's always asking what color my hair is now, and it's so hard to describe the nuances of my highlights as they grow out.

I'm getting worse too. When my publicist/agents/manager first told me to start tweeting, Instagramming, and Facebooking, I became temporarily obsessed. I remember this feeling from when I was in high school and I would go to class and everyone would be talking about a party I wasn't invited to the night before. It really sucked, and as soon as I started playing on Twitter, years and years later, those feelings came flooding back. I became obsessed with watching my number of Twitter followers grow, with who is following who, who posts what, how many followers he/she has, especially in comparison to me. It's kind of a ridiculous time suck, isn't it? I'm working on moderation in all areas of my life, but I'm an all-or-nothing kind of girl, and I needed to back off. My friends tried to warn me, but I didn't listen. I should have known. I was just as bad as my teenage stepkids—the three of us would sit on the sofa for hours thumbing our way through the Twittersphere and Instagramland. I am going to try not to judge other people for doing it, but I needed to get it under control. I liked not knowing what I was missing, but now we know everything all the time. We know where our friends are, what they are doing, who they are with, and when they are doing something that they didn't invite us to. We also know when we are dumped for something better. I get canceled on a lot (to be fair, I cancel a lot too), and now I can see/read what the canceler is doing that was better than having dinner with me. Also, I am very sensitive, and I obsessively read my followers' tweets and got really insecure when they said bad things. I needed to learn to either (a) not read anything, (b) not care (ding ding ding), or (c) quit everything and buy a lavender farm in Oregon. My mom told me when I was little that I needed to toughen up, but I didn't think I would have to rely on that advice as an adult. Shouldn't I be tough by now? I want to be beef jerky, not whipped cream. Hollywood, for me, has always felt like a popularity contest. Shouldn't this town have made my skin at least a little thicker by now? I liked it when I was living in my little bubble where the only jobs I really knew about were the ones I auditioned for or watched once they were released. I was way less insecure before I could read tweets from all of the people I was following and see how busy they were as I sat on my sofa eating an entire pizza and watching *Road House* on a Tuesday afternoon.

Speaking of popularity contests, the red carpet is just about the worst place to take a stroll if you are having a low-self-esteem day. I have been on the red carpet for projects I am *in*, and the photographers are screaming out the names of the people walking up behind me. For the premiere of *Arrested Development*, I was behind David Cross and Amber Tamblyn on the carpet, and the rows and rows of photographers were screaming for her. They

screamed, "Amber! Amber! Over here, Amber, OVER HERE!!!"
I was standing right in front of them, and their cameras were
pointed in the complete opposite direction of my face, and I was
actually *in Arrested Development*. I know Amber Tamblyn is more
famous than me, she wasn't doing anything wrong, but doesn't it
mean anything that I had acted in the TV show they were there
to report on? I am so shy on the red carpet that to have to fight for
the photographers' attention is just not my style. I'd rather just go
in, get some popcorn, and wait for the show to start.

One last thing I feel compelled to share (and will probably
regret doing so), something that totally shocked me because I
am, apparently, totally naive. Maybe you know about this, but
my friend just told me that in those magazines you read in nail
shops and hair salons, the magazines with all the blondes and
Angelina Jolie on the cover, that famous people are sometimes
paid to walk around carrying or wearing the stuff they are walking around carrying and wearing!!! Like if you see a photo of a
celeb walking down the street holding an Arby's shake, first of
all, those shakes are delicious, so celebrities should walk around
with them, but second of all, they were probably paid by Arby's to
do it. They, most likely, had their hair and makeup done too, and
I'll bet you my entire brass snail collection that there is water in
that shake cup (Smartwater because Coca-Cola has deals with
celebrities, and celebrities don't eat dairy). I know that some oft-
papped stars drive miles and miles out of their way so they can be
photographed at prearranged locations Yes, I'm whistle-blowing
here, and most likely ensuring that I will never get one of these
lucrative offers, but I couldn't believe it when I found out that
those photos weren't real, that Kim Kardashian didn't really love
(insert beverage name she was last photographed carrying here).
Yes, me dumb.

I recently read in one of my favorite beauty blogs, *Into the*

Gloss, a post about Liv Tyler (she's so cool too, by the way). She talks about how publicity and red carpets used to be different. She used to just wear something from her closet and do her own makeup for movie premieres, but with so many more paparazzi now and all the scrutiny actors are under to look perfect, it's impossible! I loved reading that; it made me nostalgic for those times, when we were all on a more even playing field. I want to go back to simpler times, when people were famous for their specific talent, when actresses looked more natural, when their faces moved, when I knew the names of the people in the magazines. Jesus, I sound a hundred years old. Sorry, I'll put away my walker and rotary telephone. I guess I just miss the times when people could just look how they looked and it was personality, talent, and charisma that mattered most, not who wore it best, because I already know the answer to that question—it's the one with the most Twitter followers.

A Day Off
on Location

MARCH 9, 2013

JAMIE MARKS IS DEAD, LIBERTY, NEW YORK

WE SHOT UNTIL LATE LAST NIGHT, SO TODAY I WOKE
up around 11:00 a.m. I didn't stand up until after 2:30 p.m. I got all
my food by crawling across my bed and reaching the mini fridge
without getting vertical at all, it's a small room, and most everything is within reaching distance of the bed. I ate Fritos for breakfast. I had hummus as a snack straight from the container using
my index finger as a utensil, and a KIND bar for lunch because I
didn't feel like walking to one of the seven fast-food options surrounding the hotel, and the Days Inn doesn't offer room service. I
was irritated because I was watching *It's Always Sunny in Philadel-
phia* on my computer and I couldn't hear the episode because the
sound of the Fritos crunching in my mouth was too loud.

Eventually, I put on the same jeans and sweater I have been

wearing for several days in a row and walked to the Liberty Diner to write. You can wear the same outfit for days on end when you're working on location because you only really wear your clothes for the drive to and from work. I ordered my usual at the diner, a Greek salad (still obsessed with feta!), no anchovies, and a side of scrambled egg whites. This is what I eat almost every day here. I wrote for a while in a booth, but mostly I just people watched. A woman was sitting near me with her two kids; one was about five and had a Mohawk. Her mom was one of the waitresses. A man came in and sat at the bar, and for some reason the Mohawked boy really wanted to sit on his lap. The boy's mom seemed to know the man and didn't act like she cared either way what her son did. A young couple came in later, the guy was dropping his lady off at work, she was a waitress there too. He sat in a booth with headphones on drinking fountain Cokes and watching her. On my way back to my hotel room I stopped by my friend Mike Potter's room. He is the makeup artist on the film. We drank Bud Light Limes, a beverage I would never have tried at home, but it's really delicious and refreshing, and there's not a lot of options at the AMPM across the street. We watched some episodes of *The Real Housewives of Orange County* and *Vanderpump Rules*. We propped his door open, and some of the cast and crew popped in and out. It was a pretty good day. I wonder how long I could live like this. I didn't work out today and don't plan to, but I might tomorrow. I should. I will try out my new Jillian Michaels DVD that I bought at Target on my day off last weekend. I also bought several new skin care products that I don't need, except maybe the face masks. I think I need to start doing more face masks.

Everyone working on the movie is staying here at the Days Inn. It's like a frat house. Most of us have our own rooms, though some people in the crew had to share. It's an indie film, and that's what you have to do sometimes if you want to work on a movie on location. Everyone wanders around the hotel like we own it—I think people even stopped locking their doors because it's just easier than getting out of bed to open it if someone knocks. Our production office is downstairs in the Starlight Ballroom. The producers found a different office when they were scouting locations before we started filming, but when they got there on the first day, it didn't have Internet, so they temporarily moved it to the Days Inn until they could find another office space, but they never did. Now they're stuck here. I think some of the office staff actually never leaves the hotel. At least there are always free snacks in the production office, so I usually grab an apple or banana and a bottle of water before going up to my room at night after work.

Shooting a movie on location is like summer camp, at least my experience of summer camp. You don't know anyone when you get there, then you become fast friends with almost everyone and wonder how you survived without them in your life, there's some structured activities (work), some free time (days off), and then it's over as quickly as it began, and you don't see or talk to any of your new best friends ever again. It's sad to think about, but this is usually just how it is. Yes, there are exceptions, those jobs where you meet a true kindred spirit and make a forever friend, but that is rare (I hope that happens with the previously mentioned Mike Potter, fingers crossed). You always have the best of intentions when the job is winding down, but when you get home, there is so much shit you have to deal with because you have been hiding out for a month or more, you try to keep in touch, but time goes by, and before you know it, you don't.

Reentry can be jarring. Trying to explain to your friends and family what all the jokes were that you shared with your fellow location campers, why you're using new phrases and who you learned them from. You probably have loads of mail to deal with too, phone calls to return, not to mention that you need to get a new job. That hunt begins as the old one is wrapping up, toward the end of your stay out of town, but if there isn't one to go directly to, you have to really hustle when you get back to civilization, and that jolts you back to reality and out of camp mode immediately.

It's hard on friends and family, too. You're usually in a different time zone, schedules don't match up, they are eating dinner when you need to go to bed or vice versa. And it's really hard for the person stuck at home doing all the mundane everyday tasks and keeping shit together while you're away doing all kinds of new things with new people that he or she has never met. It takes a big person to deal with that. While you've been gone, everyone has learned to get on without you, but now you're back, taking up space and making a mess in places that have been organized in your absence. Your friends don't feel like going over all the stories and gossip you've missed, it's all old news for them, so you feel just as left out as they do in the world you just left. Everything works itself out in a short time, but reentry can be tough for everyone.

I have worked in a lot of random locations. When I was starting out, I was hoping for exciting and exotic locales like London, the Maldives, or at least Miami. Well, my first on-location movie was shot in Kenosha, Wisconsin. I lived in a Best Western for a month and spent most of my evenings either at the Brat Stop or singing karaoke in the lobby bar. Then there was a Holiday Inn in Casa Grande, Arizona. I have no idea where I stayed in Mexicali—I never saw it in daylight. I left before sunrise every morning and returned after sunset every night. In Scottsdale the hotel was the Hotel Valley Ho. It had a funky 1950s theme, and the pool turned into a nightclub on the weekends. Very spring break–like. In Vancouver everyone stays at the Sutton Place, except once. When I was shooting *Marmaduke*, I got really lucky and got to stay at the Shangri-La, but the hotel had just opened, and the production got an insane deal. I'm convinced I'll never get to stay there again unless I pay for it. I work in New York, a lot, and have stayed in too many different hotels and apartments there to count. I lived with the entire cast of *The Village* in a bed-and-breakfast that was rented out for the shoot in rural Pennsylvania. I've worked in Lexington, Kentucky, Seattle, Las Vegas, Rhode Island, the Hamptons, Phoenix, Pittsburgh, Hawaii (finally, an exotic locale!), New Orleans, Shreveport, and Toronto. Not all so horrible, but not what I was fantasizing about when I got my SAG card.

I have learned to live in, and love, all of these cities. On my days off, I drive around them until I'm lost. I go running and see all the shops and restaurants close-up. I ask locals who look like people I would be friends with where they hang out. I look for parks and museums. I read travel guides. I rent bikes. I actually bought a bike on Craigslist last summer in Toronto because it was cheaper than renting. It's a fun adventure. Figuring out a new location, pretending I live there. Sure, I have my melodramatic homesick moments when I cry on the phone with my husband, or send long, sad e-mails to my friends back home hoping for sympathy because I'm so lonely, but I've gotten good at making new friends. Sometimes I feel like a sailor with a girl in every port, but instead I am an actress with a friend in every town.

No, my career hasn't taken me to London, Paris, or South Africa yet. Yes, I will probably purchase my next meal at a gas station while wearing pajamas under my winter coat. But all this traveling and killing time on my days off has taught me to really appreciate what I have back home. Being homesick is good—it means I am happy in my real life. That doesn't mean I don't enjoy taking off for a while, making new friends, exploring a new place, but by the end I think Dorothy got it right: there is no place like home, except maybe Hawaii.

Ashton Kutcher Gave My Dad a Harley

NO, REALLY, HE DID. I'M NOT MAKING THIS UP. IT'S not just a clever title disguising a story about something else. It happened. Ashton Kutcher gave my dad a Harley-Davidson motorcycle. I'm not totally sure why he did it, and even though I could ask him since I still work with him sometimes, he makes me nervous because he's so cute and I'm afraid I'll say something that offends him and he'll want that motorcycle back.

Here's how it happened. I was doing a TV pilot called *Miss Guided*. It was a half-hour comedy in which I played a high school guidance counselor working in the high school I attended. My character is in love with the Spanish teacher, and in the pilot episode my high school nemesis returns after a nasty divorce to teach history. Maybe it was English, I forget which, but she's superhot and threatens my budding relationship with Tim, the Spanish teacher. It made it to series for seven episodes on ABC a few years ago, premiering at 11:30 p.m. after an episode of *Dancing with the Stars*, which is historically the best time slot to showcase a new comedy (not). In addition to ABC and 20th Century

Fox, Katalyst Films produced the show. Enter Ashton Kutcher—Katalyst Films is his production company. We shot the pilot at Long Beach Polytechnic (graduates include Snoop Dogg and Cameron Diaz and many, many NFL players). We were shooting the school dance scene where I hide in the bushes and one of the students asks me if he can touch my boobs (I said no). It was late at night, and while we were waiting for the crew to finish setting up the next shot, I found myself standing next to Ashton. He asked me what I would do if ABC decided to put our show on the air. The first answer that came to mind and out of my mouth was, "I would buy my dad a Harley-Davidson motorcycle. He really wants one." Ashton looked at me and said, "If this show gets picked up, I'm going to buy your dad a Harley-Davidson motorcycle." I can't remember anything after that except Ashton staring at me and smiling.

Months and months passed with no word from ABC about the fate of our pilot, but finally it was May, the time of year when the major networks announce their fall and mid-season schedules, and *Miss Guided* was on it!! It was going to air after the holidays (mid-season) when one of their new shows failed, got canceled, and left an open time slot. That made me feel a little bad, rooting for a new show to fail, but I managed. During this time, when the networks announce their new acquisitions, they fly some of the actors, writers, and producers to New York City for a big party with advertisers called the upfronts. I call it a "dance, monkey, dance party" because it's the one time a year that the advertisers can walk around and meet all of us actors, and we are supposed to charm them so they want to pay the network to play their commercials during our TV shows. They can talk to us, have their photos taken with us, and ask for autographs, since they are technically paying our salaries. I mean it is the advertisers who pay the network for the time to air their commercials, and the network then pays us money to act in shows that fill the space between commercials. Sometimes I wonder if television shows are really just vehicles for companies to air their commercials so they can tell you what to buy, where to eat, where to donate your money, and every four years who to vote for. It's very exciting, and I was thrilled to finally be a part of it.

I started out the evening nervous about people talking to me because I get really shy at work events, but an hour and some cocktails in I was practically reaching out and grabbing people as they walked by, daring them to get a photo with me. I thought everyone would want to meet me and talk to me about my new show. That they would be doing research to find out where their ads would be best placed and would therefore want to find the best fit for their product. Yeah . . . no. I was reaching just a little. No one wanted to talk to me, and no one cared about my show. Everyone was too busy waiting in line to get some *Desperate Housewives* action. The line for getting your photo taken with the housewives or anyone from the cast of *Ugly Betty* was wrapping around the room. I think the *Grey's Anatomy* folks didn't even show up because it would have required extra security. Yeah, while VPs from Trident and Stouffer's waited for their turn to get a Polaroid with Eva Longoria, I stood under the *Miss Guided* poster, smiled, and waited. Sometimes the end of a line would snake around near my corner, and someone would grab a quick snapshot with me, just in case I turned out to be somebody after my first season aired, but mostly people would just smile encouragingly in my direction.

Just then, when I least expected anything good to come of the evening, is when it happened. Ashton's assistant walked up to me, handed me a white envelope with my name on it, and said, "This is from Ashton." I opened it immediately. It was a card that said something about dreams coming true on the front, blah

blah blah, but inside the card was a photo of a Harley, and on the photo it said, "Call this number to arrange pickup."

WHAT. THE. FUCK.

I was speechless. Like, totally speechless. I still am kind of. Wait, pick up what? *That motorcycle?* The next twenty minutes are a bit of a blur, I might have blacked out for a minute, my brain was spinning out of control. I had to find Ashton right away, but the party tent was so huge, and crowded, it felt like it took up a whole New York City block. Where was he?! I left my post and started frantically searching for him, I knew he'd be surrounded by people, so I tried to pay attention to clusters as opposed to lines of people. When I found him, I remember getting so overwhelmed with nerves and questions. Why did he do this? How do I thank him for this? What do I tell people? Is it a secret, or can I stand on top of the bar and make a grand announcement? I was sure if I smashed a bottle of Absolut, I could get everyone to shut up for fifteen seconds and pay attention to me. I had scattered just-got-motorcycle-for-dad brain, but I remember finding him standing with people and me waiting a few seconds to get his attention, him noticing me standing there holding the card, him smiling, me stammering, my mouth moving and sounds coming out, and tears. I wanted to pull him aside, away from everyone he was entertaining, and say, "Thank you, but why? Why this? Why me? How can I ever repay this? I don't deserve this, my dad does, but I don't. How do I make it so I deserve this?" But I didn't get the chance. And I didn't necessarily get the sense that Ashton Kutcher wanted to have a heart-to-heart with me about it in front of all those people he was talking to. And I was afraid I would embarrass him because I could barely hold back tears. I am not used to random acts of kindness. Occasionally, people will let me cut in line at the market if I only have one or two items and they have a cart full, but this, this was a whole different ball game.

And Ashton is a celebrity! And he barely even knew me. How did he know I would appreciate it? Does he do this all the time? I was so confused by his generosity.

Needless to say, my father was in total shock when it was delivered to his house in Ohio. I arranged it with my mom so it would be a surprise. I wasn't there when it was delivered, because I was shooting 27 *Dresses* in Rhode Island. But much like me, he was blown away. My dad rides that motorcycle starting the first nice day in the spring and waits until the last possible moment in winter to put it away. He is obsessed.

Oddly, I also think it's helped my parents' marriage. Before the Harley, my parents would argue most about the boat they owned. My father insisted on buying one, which, as my mom predicted, sat in the garage all year, save for one day in the summer when my family would get their shit together enough to pull it out, hook it up to the back of my dad's truck, drag it to some nearby lake, spend twenty-five minutes backing it in at the boat launch, try to start it for about forty-five minutes, and, when it wouldn't, pull it out again and drive home. These excursions were stressful, but I usually got some kind of awesome ice cream sundae out of them, and the lake was pretty to look at, even if we seldom made it in. But after the Harley showed up, my dad sold the boat. The Harley lives in the garage where the boat used to, and it starts every time he turns the key. He can drive it right down the driveway and on the road to start his adventure. So, in a roundabout way, Ashton also kind of saved my parents' marriage. That might be a *little* hyperbolic, but he did help end a thirty-plus-year argument. Maybe next Ashton could help my dad get the taxes turned in on time.

For years I saved all the fortunes from all the fortune cookies I got at restaurants and from takeout. I had loads of them. One day I sat down and sorted through them all and took out the good ones. I taped them to a piece of paper and sent them to Ashton Kutcher. I wanted him to have all the good fortune I felt the universe had planned for me, because I already had all I could handle. Sometimes, for no reason at all, someone does something unbelievable, unselfish, and generous. I really hope he reads this because I still feel like I've never properly thanked him for his kindness, so if you're reading this, I'd just like to say . . . Thank you, Fairy God–Ashton, you made the sweetest man out there and his undeserving daughter so very, very happy.

Intolerance

YOU KNOW HOW CELEBRITIES HAVE THEIR OWN PER-
fumes these days? Well, I don't know if I'm a real celebrity, but I, Judy Greer, want my own perfume. I have the scent picked out and everything. There was an oil that the Body Shop discontinued years ago called Mostly Musk. My friend Sarah turned me on to it, and when my first bottle was just about gone, I went to buy a second, only to find out that the company no longer made it. I had heard that a friend of a friend once called the Bonne Bell 800 number in an attempt to buy whatever was left of her favorite discontinued grape-flavored lip balm, and they sold her the last case of it from their warehouse, and just like that, she became a grape lip-balm millionaire. I appealed to the salesgirl at the Body Shop, asking for headquarters contact information, but she was of no help, staring blankly at me and muttering, "I don't . . . know . . ." Clearly this girl was not working there while putting herself through med school, and I was never able to track down a leftover case of Mostly Musk oil. Although the fantasy of re-creating that scent is appealing, it isn't really why I want my own fragrance. The point is the name . . . and to follow through with an idea, which admittedly isn't usually my strong suit.

I came up with the name in New York City a few years ago.

I was doing a play and had lost my voice, so I was taking steroids. Seriously. I wasn't on them to bulk up, I swear. Anyway, the theater sent me to a fancy doctor on the Upper East Side. There were photos of Pavarotti on all of the walls, so either she was a *really* big fan or she was his personal throat doctor. Judging by the bill I received, which cost more than my paycheck for the entire run of the play, I gather she was the latter. So, Pavarotti's doctor gave me a giant shot of steroids in the ass, and by the time I got back to work after my appointment, I was speaking easily again. For the next week, I had to take these pills that were meant to wean me off the high-dosage shot. By the way, if you ever see me stomping down the sidewalks of N.Y.C. wearing nothing but a tank top and jean shorts in the middle of January, screaming at people for texting while walking, you'll know this: I am in a play and I have lost my voice, and it's not a good time to ask what you know me from.

So, in my juiced-up frenzy that week, a lady cut in front of me in line at Starbucks. I was on a ten-minute break from rehearsals, and I *needed* that coffee, and this bitch was not going to fuck it up for me (no, I am not currently taking the steroids). I was going to therapy that winter, and there is only one thing I can remember from all of those costly sessions: when my therapist asked, "Judy, why are you so intolerant?" She said I seemed absolutely incapable of saying "whatever" or "who cares" about most people I met and most situations I found myself in. This was before *Curb Your Enthusiasm*, which set a different tone culturally. Now it's almost preferred to be obsessed with forcing people to live by one's own moral code. My therapist was, and is, right, but I left her before I was able to figure out how to say the words she wanted me to say, in the order she wanted me to say them.

So, this was the birth of Intolerance. And I am officially announcing it in this book: my perfume will be called "Intolerance, for the woman who just can't take it anymore." It's inspired by bad drivers, people who don't use their left-hand turn signal, people who don't use their right-hand turn signal, tardy friends, line cutters, slow (or worse, chatty) checkout clerks, music playing while on hold, faulty DVRs, airplane seat kickers, airplane seat headrest grabbers, loud cell-phone talkers, text-and-walkers, people who don't silence their phone in the theater, and L.A. traffic. Intolerance is also inspired by my own shortcomings. By my hatred for, and inability to do, my own hair, by the famous people who have landed the roles I have auditioned and was right for, by my lack of self-discipline, by the rate at which my nails grow versus the amount of time I can carve out for manicures, by my inability to have just one slice of pizza. And, of course, no rant is any good without some hatred allotted for big-picture problems: the state of our environment; the hungry people in our own country, and all over the world; the rich people getting richer, and the poor people staying just as poor; people who are cruel to animals; bullies; and a good education costing so much money, to name just a few.

I have been intolerant for years, but the idea for a perfume about it started with some prednisone and a bitch in Starbucks. So when it's the holidays and you buy a prepackaged gift set of accompanying bath gel and body butter hopefully smelling like Mostly Musk from the Body Shop, remember that sometimes being intolerant can be a good thing, it can bring about change. Spray some on your wrist and, to quote one of my favorite movies, get mad as hell, and don't take it anymore! I'm selling the idea that we might not *have* to take it anymore. We can try, spritz by spritz, to be the change we want to see happen. I'm not just selling a perfume, I'm selling a movement, but don't worry, this movement will smell delicious.

The Tortoise
and the Hare

SLOW AND STEADY WINS THE RACE. THAT'S HOW I'VE always thought of my career, like the fable "The Tortoise and the Hare." When I started out, I was one of hundreds of girls starting their acting careers. Some girls saw a lot of success right away, and some (me) got smaller roles but a steady amount of them. At first I found myself being jealous of girls who were cast in great roles, even though it seemed all they did was look perfect. I wondered how I could ever compete. I thought there was something I was missing—maybe it was my look, maybe it was my acting, I didn't know, but at the time I felt I was missing something. Now, fifteen years later, I see it differently. No, I have yet to become a movie or TV star, but I have never stopped working. I have worked steadily this whole time, and I'm busier than ever. I don't even know what a lot of those other girls are up to. I don't know if they are working, if they've given up, or maybe they grew up with a trust fund and didn't really need to work that hard in the first place (I've always fantasized about a trust fund). Now, I am in no way saying that I am a better actress than any of them, or a better person, and I am for sure not better looking, but for whatever reason I am still working. I'm working harder than ever, and I am still excited about becoming a better actress, working with great people, and challenging myself. I make a good living, I didn't spend all my money when I first made it, I *wanted* to but didn't—I have been (mostly) careful. I have saved. I have been cheap. I have also tried to be nice to people, listen to advice, and not take anything for granted. It will always be hard to watch actresses play roles that I auditioned for and really wanted, I still get jealous and, if I've had too many glasses of wine, bitter. I get momentarily jealous (OK, maybe it lasts a wee bit longer than a moment) when I see people come out of nowhere and become sensations, as if they were shot through a cannon. Did I miss an announcement saying where to line up for the cannon shooting? I still audition. I still write letters to directors asking them to please cast me. I wonder if I will ever get tired of trying to convince people that I can do it, and stop trying so hard.

Most of the time I am happy with where I am. I am grateful every day about something, and I am excited about all the things that I get to do because I don't have to worry that much about what it will do for my career, because my career is a little bit of everything. I'm diversified. I don't have to worry about maintaining some status or level of fame, because what I do has been so varied. Not being a movie star has been the greatest freedom, it turns out. Sir Isaac Newton said, "An object in motion stays in motion," and I remember learning in acting school that "work begets work," so I have always just tried to stay in motion and keep working.

I used to think about where I wanted my career to go. I made specific goals for myself and tried to achieve them. But I don't know about goals as much anymore. I am finding more and more that I feel better when I let things come to me. I don't get as down when I don't get what I want. That's not to say that I don't try to push myself—I'm pretty driven and competitive—but I have learned that for me it's a marathon, not a sprint. I have always been a late bloomer. I don't have a clear picture of where I see myself in ten years, five, even one year. Alive, I hope, but that's about it. I really love people. I love being on a set. I love solving problems. As an actor, you don't get to solve a lot of problems; you're not asked to that often. You don't have much control over anything. You are told what to do, and you do it. You're often asked what feels right, and sometimes you get manipulated into thinking that a decision was yours, but at the end of the day (directors say that a lot) it's not ultimately up to you, at least that's been my experience so far. So, in the future, it might be fun to have more control. I produced a TV pilot, and it was awesome. It was network television, so I really only had the illusion of control, but I liked the feeling of the illusion. It was fun to be asked what I thought, and it was fun to problem solve.

But there is a fear. A new feeling I have now that I haven't had before. The fear of it all ending and regretting having wasted any small opportunity I might have had. Of what happens next. Of not appreciating the experiences, of not getting to go shoot movies anymore. I love it. I love making something out of nothing. It's taken years for me to call myself an artist, and even as I write it, I'm not sure I believe that word describes what I do. I say words that other people write. I act in a space that other people find, build, and decorate. I wear clothes that someone else picks out, I don't even do my own hair and makeup. I could even argue that I don't make any choices for my character, depending on the director. I just talk and try to remember what to say. Acting is weird. I guess my art is being a mirror to people. I show them a person. Maybe themselves, maybe someone they know. I help tell a story so when you see it from the outside, you can understand your insides better. I also make you forget. Forget your shitty day, week, month, year, for a little while. That's important, right? I give people a memory. Is it the movie we love or the memory of when we watched it? For years my family watched *Planes, Trains, and Automobiles* on Christmas Eve, and that movie will always mean so much to me. Or when you have a movie you love with another person. My mom and I love *The American President*, and when I go home for a visit, we always watch it—it's "our" movie. She makes us popcorn and we quote it and it makes us feel connected. Maybe having a movie or TV show is like having a song when you're a couple. I am working with this young actor right now who says he watches *Two and a Half Men* with his dad when they want to have some laughs. That makes me happy. It made me happy when the actor told me his dad was excited he was doing a movie with me because his dad associated me with laughing and having fun with his son. I like the idea that I can be a part of bringing people together. But does that make me an artist? I am working on believing it does. I've just always thought of what I did as a job. Maybe it's my midwestern work ethic, but I never used to think of jobs as something I could choose, I let jobs choose me. Maybe that's the difference between being an actress and being an artist. I am envious of my friends who make distinct choices in their careers. That they won't play certain roles anymore, to do theater, to only do movies, to take themselves out of the game in some way, seems so decisive and punk rock. I feel boring when I compare myself with them. But that is my fear talking again, and being afraid it will all go away if I change my tactics now.

Maybe I'm afraid of being broke, maybe I am afraid of change. The first time I can remember not taking a role that was offered to me was when I got serious with my husband, before we were married. He said I shouldn't take that job, that I could wait for something better to come along, and if I needed money, he would help me figure it out. I have never had anyone offer that before. It felt really good to have someone tell me it was OK if I didn't work on something that I wasn't excited about. I'm not going to say what the job was, but it rhymes with "separate mouseflies." I think since then my fear-based decision making is slowly subsiding, and I am getting a little more bold with my choices. I am learning to look for people to inspire me.

I had an acting teacher, Eden Cooper-Sage, who told me, "We are what we spend our time doing," and I want so badly to be an artist, so how can I transition from spending my time acting to spending my time making art? Or is it really one and the same? I like working and maybe it's as simple as that. I am like the turtle in that stupid race. I may be slow, but I think I'm winning. Winning changes, and now, as I get older, I understand winning doesn't mean what I thought it did. I am not a shooting co-star. I am a bright co-star, a steady co-star, a co-star you can depend on if you're lost, flipping channels in the night. Except if you stumble on *Marmaduke*, that was purely a money gig.

Part 3

Real Life

Single White Male

male has been eight years, and it's still going strong. He is everything to me. He's extremely masculine and has a sexy swagger and a really judgmental stare. I love the judgment, it appeals to the part of me that likes bad boys. He's also very tired, which makes us a great match because so am I, and I tend to overbook and leave little time for our long walks. Yes, his teeth are falling out, but I don't hold it against him. In fact, I think he still looks handsome without them. He doesn't know this, but I keep them in my jewelry box. I don't know what I'm ever going to do with them, but I have a friend who is a jewelry designer, so I am considering having a few dipped in gold and turned into a necklace or something. I think that would make me really happy, to have some of him with me all the time.

If you haven't already realized, I'm not some freak talking about her lazy, toothless ex-boyfriend (I wrote about that guy in a different chapter. Just kidding!). I'm talking about Buckley, my giant white American bulldog. The day I picked him up from the rescue, I almost changed my mind. He was bigger than I remembered, like way bigger. When I first met him, it was at a pet rescue outside a pet store, and he was sick and had been hit by a car, so he was lying down and couldn't stand up. The Dog Rescue Lady had given him about eighteen pig ears to chew on, and the smell that was coming out of his asshole was otherworldly. I was entertaining the idea of taking home a petite pit mix named Jessie and had dragged my then boyfriend, Nick, to meet her. We were looking at Jessie when an odor wafted our way. It was thick. I had never experienced such a thick odor before. It was also rich—thick and rich is really the best way to describe it. When I asked said Dog Rescue Lady what the smell was, she pointed to Bucks and said, "It's the big one in the corner. He's sick and I am giving him pig ears nonstop to fatten him up." When we walked over to him, he looked up at me and smiled, I swear.

Nick and I were on our way to lunch with his family, so we didn't have a real conversation about the smelly dog in the corner. But halfway through the meal, we both admitted we couldn't stop thinking about that giant stinker. As soon as we got home, we called the rescue, arranged the house checks, filled out a shit-ton of paperwork, gave him another week to mend, and I went to pick him up. When I saw Bucks for the second time, I was kind of freaked out. I didn't remember him being so big, because I had never seen him standing up. He was freaking huge—like the size of a baby cow or small tiger. He even walks like a small tiger. The cost of rescuing the dog was two hundred dollars, but Dog Rescue Lady waived the fee because he was so sick that she said we were going to spend a fortune on vet bills so we could just have him for free. Free giant dog! Rad!

When I finally brought Buckley home, he limped out of my car, up the steps, through the house to the backyard, and all the way to the far end of the yard, where he just sat, staring at me. He didn't sniff around, he didn't pee on anything, he just walked as far away from the door as physically possible, sat, and stared. That was the beginning, and he has been judging me ever since.

He judges me when I drink too much wine. He judged who I brought home, what I wore out, when I danced to Madonna and played dress up before going to bed. He judged me when I broke up with Nick and when I started dating the new one. And all over again when I broke up with that new one. He judges when I cry at commercials, movies, books, dropping a pen. For a while after that breakup with Nick, I was convinced Buckley was depressed. My therapist told me I was projecting and there was no way that Buckley was depressed, but I could bring him in if I felt I needed to. I didn't. I had to draw the line somewhere, I can't be the girl who brings her dog to therapy, it's a slippery slope, one day I'm bringing my dog to therapy, the next, I'm pushing two sweater-clad pugs around in a baby carriage. Besides, it's nice to have that judgment I am always using on myself personified, or canine-ified, if you will. It means that I don't have to work so hard reflecting and disapproving of my own actions and decisions. I can just look over at him after making them; he does the judging for me.

But even with all that judgment, he is loving and downright human when he wants to be. One time, a vet sat down on the ground to examine him—there was no way we were getting him up on that table—and my giant dog turned his back to the vet and sat right on his lap. The vet was at first silent and then finally said, "I've never had an animal do this before." He loves to ride in the car with his head out the window. I've heard that's bad for dogs, but he loves it so much, and I know we won't be together forever, so shouldn't he get to do what he loves with his short time on earth? He used to sleep in bed with me (pre-husband), with his head on the pillow, like a person. He stretches his shoulders by pushing his front paws together so it looks like he's praying. One time we were watching TV together on the sofa. He was sitting up next to me facing the television, just like me. After a particularly stupid scene he looked at me, took a deep breath, held it, opened his mouth, as if he were going to say something . . . but then finally exhaled and turned his head back to the TV. I swear on everything, including him, that he was going to talk to me. I know he had something to say. Something major. Some kind of insight that would change my life. But, shit, even if he said, "This show sucks," it would change my life. I would become the girl who swears her dog can talk. Which, who am I kidding, I kind of am anyway because I have pretty much told everyone I know this story, swearing that he *can* talk, but just decided I wasn't ready yet.

As I said, I brought him home and he just sat there, staring. This went on for about three months. I bought him a dog bed from L.L.Bean with his name embroidered on it. I figured he should at least be comfortable while he sat and stared. He seemed to like the bed, but he still didn't do much of anything. He was too busted to go on walks, so we just let him lie there. He didn't move except to eat, which was great, I guess. I had promised his rescuer I would cook him ground beef and rice for his meals every day while he healed. Which I did. I had never cooked a real meal in my life, but here I was cooking beef and rice every day for my new-to-me dog, trying to fatten him up. One time I mixed some broccoli florets in with his meal, and when he finished eating, I noticed all his food was gone. I was so thrilled he ate his veggies, until I bent down to pick up his dog bowl and saw that he had picked out every piece of broccoli and made a neat little pile of it next to the bowl. You see, Bucky had a hard life. He was found roaming the streets of East Los Angeles with a little Chihuahua. The dogcatcher brought them into the pound and put them in a cage together, which was the protocol when they catch a pair of dogs. Buckley's rescuer specializes in American bulldogs, so all the local shelters call her first when they pick one up. She told them she would be in the next day to get the two dogs, and in the amount of time it took for them to finish that phone call, the

Chihuahua died. They called her back and said never mind, the bulldog had killed the Chihuahua, and it was their policy to put any dog to sleep that had killed another dog, they had no choice. Dog Rescue Lady freaked out and said, "Wait! Did you examine the Chihuahua? Does it have broken bones or puncture marks? How do you know it was killed? Maybe it just died." She convinced them to X-ray the little dead dog and check it for puncture wounds. She was right! There was no evidence of malice on the Chihuahua, and Buckley's life was spared! However, at this time Buckley started to show signs of illness. He wasn't able to walk well at all (it was decided he had been hit by a car), and when Dog Rescue Lady had her favorite vet, Dr. Werber, neuter him, Buckley started to bleed to death during the surgery. Turns out Buckley and his little friend were poisoned. A lot of restaurants put rat poison in their garbage, and a lot of stray dogs die from it. That poor Chihuahua was so little it died almost immediately, but Buckley is so big it took longer to invade his system, and that's why he didn't get as sick right away. Dr. Werber somehow stopped the bleeding and Buckley hung on, but it was touch and go there for a while. He lived at the animal hospital while they nursed him back to health. He was too skinny, he limped and needed a few more operations to clear out the damaged cartilage in his shoulder, but he was ready for a permanent home. Once I heard that story, I knew he had to be mine, and I understood why the rescue was taking such precautions with this creature and why I had to fill out more paperwork to adopt him than when I bought my house. They were taking no chances, he was special, he was exonerated, a prisoner sentenced to death row for a crime he didn't commit, and I was waiting at the jailhouse gate when he was released.

It took a while for Buckley to feel at home in our house, personalized dog bed or not; it seemed he was just going to keep sleeping until he got moved to a different place again. I worried that he would never assimilate, that I would never be able to make him feel safe and loved. Until one day, I ordered pizza *a lot*, and I would just leave the front door wide open and the pizza guy would usually just walk up to the door and say hi and I'd come running at him with a fistful of cash. The first time the pizza guy saw Bucky lying on his dog bed in the house, he reacted with an "oh, shit," but when my massive beast didn't budge, he wasn't scared. Well, about three months in, the delivery guy showed up and Buckley stood up on his bed and barked. Really barked. I had never heard that sound before, so I came running. This time there was an all-caps "OH, SHIT" out of the delivery guy, and when I saw Buckley protecting the house and me in it, I was touched. I was really moved. I probably even cried a little, because that was the moment I could finally tell that Buckley knew he was home, and this was where he was staying.

He lived a rough life on the Eastside. He was poisoned, hit by a car, maybe even shot—he has some weird scars. He still flinches sometimes when I reach to pet him, but at least since that day he barked at the pizza guy, he's known he was here to stay. And I have always felt his presence made my house a home. It was hard to have people over at times, if Buckley's stomach was acting up. If a date was dropping me off, I would have to go in alone first before inviting him in for a nightcap, just in case the smell was too putrid and it would reflect poorly on me. The girls in my book club would often request that he relax in the bedroom or out on the deck during our meetings. He farts audibly, belches out loud, and leaves a trail of coarse white hairs everywhere he goes. But it was always a good gauge. Could a date handle the other man in my life? Would Buckley turn his back as a sign of submission or just sit and stare in judgment? Would my book club demand a different location? How irritated would a new friend be requesting a lint brush before leaving my house? Buckley has a lot of qualities that I admire in a person. He's mellow, likes to be outside, but is happy to just sit and watch TV as well. He is a good listener, honest, enjoys a good meal, patient, and he really likes to stop and smell the roses, literally. Who would have thought that eight years ago a dog fart would change my life, but it did, and in the best possible way.

Love Not at First Sight

HOW DO YOU WRITE ABOUT BEING SO IN LOVE WITH someone that you cry almost every day because you can't believe it happened to you and you are so happy and you love him so much . . . without making people vomit their last four meals up? (I'm crying right now, by the way.) This is the most difficult essay to write because every time I think about it I cry and can't see the computer screen. Also, I can't write it in public, because people stare and ask me if I'm OK and it's embarrassing. Are you vomiting yet? I don't blame you. It's annoying. I would be annoyed, too. In fact, I am often annoyed because the fact that I cry about it all the time has really been a problem. Disclaimer: I'm a crier. I have always been tear prone. I cry at auditions when I am not supposed to cry. I cry driving, *a lot*, I cry at the movies, I cry at commercials, I cry describing movies or commercials. The second season of *Grey's Anatomy*? *Forget it!* I was a mess for weeks. You get it. It's constant and a daily activity for me. However, since I met Dean Johnsen, it's gotten really out of control. I can't even use my tears for manipulative purposes with him anymore, because he's immune. Everyone in my life is immune at this point. I get further by not crying. Still barfing?

I have tried to figure out why I have this reaction to my relationship. I have always been emotional, but this is different. I don't know exactly what to blame it on besides Dean Johnsen coming out of the woodwork and taking me by surprise. But it was a slow surprise, like if you walked into a surprise party and it took the guests a few months to yell the word "surprise."

I don't believe in love at first sight. Love at first sight has historically gotten me in a lot of trouble. I have had long relationships that should have been one-night stands because of "love at first sight." It's not really love. How can you love someone you don't even know? It's chemistry, it's hormones, it's that time of the month, but it's not love. I wish someone would've told me that—OK, a lot of people told me that, I just didn't listen. But I spent a lot of time with men trying to get that feeling back after more sights. Or trying to justify jumping into a relationship because I wanted that feeling to be real, or I wanted it to mean something, or mostly because I didn't want to feel like a slut. And I must have subconsciously figured that if I jumped into a relationship with a guy and then realized I'd made a mistake, I would be able to justify the mistake by saying it was something bigger than either of us—it was the universe, the gods, not Ketel One.

The second mistake I made over and over again was not believing people when they told me that relationships should be easy. My mom told me when I was younger that relationships were work, but I took her literally. She was telling me this in response to people she knew getting divorced without working on their marital problems first. I know now that she was trying to teach me to be a good partner, a team player. She meant you have to work at keeping relationships good and healthy and strong, not that you had to work to make a bad relationship good. Oops.

People ask Dean and me all the time if it was love at first sight when we met, if we just "knew" because we met on a blind date and are so perfect for each other. Together and separately we both give the same answer every time. No. I remember so vividly the moment I first saw Dean Johnsen. It wasn't on Facebook, I don't have that. Or Instagram, or Twitter, or even MySpace, Friendster, or the microfiche at the local library. It was the old-fashioned, 100-percent blind-date way. When I opened the front door. He was tall. He was handsome. He smiled brightly, and his eyes were happy. He seemed nice. Did my stomach do flips? No. Did I feel like I was having an out-of-body experience? No. Was I excited that he had a bottle of wine in his hand? YES.

We had a totally normal first date. A predinner glass of wine on my deck, where we discussed different landscaping options (yawn) while Buckley sat next to Dean panting and staring, never taking his eyes off him for a second. Then we went to dinner at a loud, dark sushi restaurant and tried to make small talk, but it was too loud and too dark. When we finished dinner, we both had to use the bathroom before leaving, which was down a hallway that was even darker than the restaurant. The ladies' room was just as dark as the hallway, and my eyes never really adjusted as I waited in the hallway for Dean to come out. There was a man standing there waiting for his date, just staring at me. I stared back for a second, but I quickly gave an uncomfortable smile and looked away, nervous Dean would come out of his bathroom and see me staring at another man in the hallway and be offended. But Dean was taking forever. All this time I could have been primping, I thought. I hurried so I didn't seem like the kind of girl who took forever in the ladies' room, even though I am totally that kind of girl. I was starting to get worried. What if he was allergic to something I ordered and was really sick? What if he went to the valet to get the car? Wait, what did we agree on? Was I supposed to wait in the hall for him? Or were we to meet at the valet stand? What if he left altogether because I was screaming all through dinner because it was so loud? Shit. And as this was all running through my head, this guy was still staring at me. "Fine," I thought, "I can stare too." Finally, the guy said, "Should we go?" SHIT! Shit, shit, shit, that is my date! Did I actually forget what my date looked like, even though I have been staring at his face for the last two hours? Yes. I squeaked out a "Sure. You?" And Dean answered, "Yes. Unless you want to hang out in this hallway longer?" "No, I'm good," I said. We walked. I cringed.

For the record, I would have gone out for a nightcap with him anyway, but after that debacle there was no way I was ending the night there. It was the Guinness across the street that finally loosened us up. About a year later I told Dean about that moment in the hallway and was thrilled to find out he was having the same panic attack I was! I guess the whole concept of love at first sight kind of slipped us by, considering that neither of us had any idea who we were staring at on our first date anyway.

A book I read once quoted a man saying, "It wasn't love at first sight, but it is now." And I always think of that when people ask me about that first blind date. I really had no idea what he looked like, but after getting to know him on the phone for a few weeks prior, I decided it didn't really matter. I liked talking to him on the phone. He made me laugh uncontrollably before we even met, and when I saw his number on my caller ID I picked up, no matter what. Still do, actually. Yes, when I opened my front door and he seemed clean and didn't look like he had a record, I was pleased, but honestly I would have been excited to go out with him anyway.

When I say that realizing I was in love with him snuck up on me, I really mean it. I just found myself making room for him in my schedule. I wanted to tell him good news first, and I wasn't embarrassed to tell him the bad stuff. He was easy and fun to hang out with. We didn't fight. He made me laugh really hard every time we spoke on the phone. He wasn't jealous or competitive with me. He never judged. He was the first real grown-up I had ever dated, and it was easy. But the aha moment was when I was talking to my friend Sean about him and Sean said, "You know how I know he's the one? Because you've never asked me what I think about him. Because for the first time you don't care." Aha.

I told Dean I loved him for the first time waiting in line to use the bathroom at a restaurant in Austin, Texas, it seemed like the perfect place, it was another dark hallway, but this time I knew exactly who I was talking to.

Drugstore Therapy

night trip to a twenty-four-hour drugstore couldn't give me at least a few moments of calm and clarity. I began my drugstore therapy in earnest during college. I lived dangerously close to a twenty-four-hour Walgreens, and my roommates and I spent many nights procrastinating on our schoolwork by scouring the shelves for some late-night beauty inspiration. It is where Janet and I would buy fashion magazines, which would then inspire another trip out to purchase the items required to make us look exactly like the models on the pages. It didn't always work (tip: don't try to dye your hair from brown to platinum blond using a box of hair bleach, or at least don't let Janet do it), but we had fun, and who cares if my hair turned pink and orange? We were in college. My life was easier then, when my issues weren't as big, but even now, while my problems are getting grander in scope, a new tube of lipstick or a travel-size body lotion still has the power to lighten my stress load a considerable amount. I've had this experience to a lesser degree at malls in the past, and trust me, if there was a mall open at 11:00 p.m., I'd probably hit that up too. But shopping decisions are bigger at malls, and I'm safer on a smaller scale. If I hate my lipstick the next day, it's a less costly retail mistake than buying a new dress.

Maybe it's the aimless wandering under the fluorescent lights or the hopefulness that a new pack of pens promises. I'm not really sure, but CVS might just be my happy place. And not because of the abundance of ice cream and candy bars; in fact, I don't usually buy food. Usually. For me, the draw is the products. Skin care, makeup, hair accessories . . . I am wired to believe that somewhere in those aisles the solution to my problem will be found. A new bottle of Nivea might make the girl who got the part I auditioned for pass on it. Revlon's Orange Flip lipstick could very well make my ex-boyfriend fall down a flight of stairs (where he would turn up injured, not dead, jeez, I'm not that evil). Even a three-pack of Pilot fine-point pens purchased at 1:00 a.m. will probably make the network decide to pick up my pilot, or at least make some footage that was never filmed miraculously turn up in the editing room. WHAT? THESE THINGS COULD HAPPEN!

OK, I know they will not happen, but there is something about a late-night drugstore run that promises change, and in these moments, all I *really* want is change. I want to not have the problem I am having. I want to be a different person, and maybe if I were different, my problem would be solved, or better yet, not exist at all. If I were cleaner, if my nails were Revlon Red, if my hair was coated in Moroccan oil, if I used Cetaphil to wash my face, as all dermatologists recommended and all celebrities claimed they did in the magazines also purchased in these late-night runs, my life would be hassle-free. I even went on my wedding day, although this trip was *not* to solve a problem, or to check out for a while, it was to savor a few stolen moments with my girls before the wedding would take over the day, as weddings tend to do. Everyone was telling me to steal a few moments with my groom during the reception, but what about my best friends? And what better place to do it than in the Walgreens across from the hotel? Besides, I "needed" some face wash before I walked down the aisle, duh. I bought all of their favorite products, and while I used them up in the following months I thought of Janet, Kelly, and me walking up and down the aisles talking about our favorite lotions—not that I was about to walk down a more serious aisle at 5 p.m. that evening. We bonded and I felt calm and excited for this next stage of my life. For a while, my trips got a little crazy. I was producing and starring in a TV pilot about my life, and every night before I went home, I told my husband I had to "run an errand," which was code for a drugstore run. He knew it, I didn't need a code, but there was also an element of secrecy that I needed from it too. I didn't want to be running a real errand; I wanted to be selfish about my trip. I wanted it to be my secret place where I could lose myself in whatever was catching my eye. Not on a mission for Ziploc baggies for tomorrow's school lunches, I wanted to wander, I wanted to discover, I wanted to silence my phone, be by myself, and think of nothing. I don't know how else to describe this to a man, except to say it's my sports.

While I was shooting my pilot, every day, without fail, something would happen that was completely out of my control, and I needed to get that back. The network throws out the whole script days before we start production? St. Ives Apricot Scrub. We can't find an actor to play my husband? A pack of black Goody no-break hair elastics and a leopard-print nail file. The cut isn't working and our editor refuses to scour through the footage to find more options? Neutrogena makeup remover wipes, Burt's Bees lip balm, CoverGirl NatureLuxe lip shine, and Aveeno shave cream. The day after that particular drugstore run, the editor still seemed to hate me, and the pilot hadn't changed one bit, but when I got there in the morning, my lips were a pretty color, my face was superclean, my legs were shaved, and I was ready to start solving some problems. It was all I could control that night, and no matter how shallow I may sound, it helped me sleep a little better too.

For a while I had a new partner in crime for my late-night habit, my stepdaughter, Emilee. She was usually game, no matter how much homework she had. Maybe it's because she knew I would pay, or maybe she really did need more conditioner, but if that were the case, wouldn't she just ask me to pick some up for her? I could see the twinkle in her eye while we were parking the car. And like me, she prefers to shop alone. We would wait for the glass doors to part and go our separate ways until we felt ready to face the world again. But now that she can drive herself, she doesn't need me to take her anymore, she goes alone, which is really how it should be. I don't know if she picked up the habit from me or her mom, or maybe it's just in all our lady genes, but I am confident the therapy will serve her well in the future. And if she did get it from me, I'm thrilled I could teach her something of real value.

Dear Laura A. Moses:
A Letter to a Friend

Dear Laura A. Moses,

I'd like to start by saying I really like you. In a platonic way, but still, a lot. I am so thankful that we met while shooting Playing for Keeps *(I still prefer the original title). I have great memories of making that movie because of you and Biel. The "Shreve" will always be a place that I remember fondly. Swimming in the pool at your rental, the alligator in the middle of the road when I drove home one night, lunches on the dock at base camp, it was really fun! You have become a really great friend to me, and I am so thankful to you for introducing me to Transcendental Meditation and Lynn. I hope you and I can visit your hometown of Fairfield, Iowa, one day—I'm dying to go there after hearing all your stories. You are a real inspiration. You're smart, witty, and beauti-ful. You have such great style and can talk me into or out of anything, that's how much I trust you. I look up to you in so many ways. I feel you have a strong moral compass and an original outlook on life.*

Do you remember that Friday night when you were coming home from work in New York and we spur-of-the-moment met for happy hour at Little Dom's? That night was so fun! I got to see your amazing apartment, and you lent me your cute Nikes? Remember? The next day was April 20, Record Store Day, and Dean Johnsen rented a party bus for his record club? Remember? You told me I should wear your shoes that day because they are so cute and perfect for party-bus record shopping. The Nike Dunk Sky Hi wedges, navy with white flecks? Well, I did wear them the next day, just like you told me to. I always listen to you, and you were right again, they are the best shoes ever! So cute and comfortable, and the navy is perfect. Really elongates the leg when worn with skinny blue jeans. I decided early in the day I had to buy a pair for myself, so did my friend Jackie. I planned on ordering them online that night!

The party bus was so fun! As you can probably imagine, we drank a lot. There was a lot of beer on the bus, we had a driver and a killer playlist playing while we did our record store hop, we even stopped to do shots between stores! Oh my God, we found the coolest bar—so dark and old-school, you would love it. We should totally go there sometime, even though I don't exactly remember where it was. I have no idea how many beers I had between 9:00 a.m. and 2:00 p.m., but, like, a lot. You know how when you drink a lot of beer, you have to pee a lot? Right? Well, there was no bathroom on the bus and not really any bathrooms in any of the record stores we stopped in. We all peed in the cool bar where we did the shots, but, man, by the time we got back to the parking garage where the bus picked us up, I had to pee like a race pony . . . again! Of course there wasn't a bathroom anywhere there either, so we all took turns peeing behind

*bushes, Dumpsters, etc. Can you believe that? How old am
I, twenty-three? Right? When was the last time you squatted
and peed in public? On concrete? Every time I do it, I swear
I'm never going to do it again, because you know how when
you pour liquid on concrete it splatters? I mean, it splatters a
lot when you're standing a few feet away from the concrete,
so you can imagine, or probably remember, how much it
splatters when you're squatting down, peeing on it, just a few
inches away from the ground. It splatters a lot. Well . . . so
think about where your feet are in relation to where the pee
splatters when you're squatting down like that. Yeah, your
feet are right there, getting splattered with pee. So gross, and
your shoes get covered in pee . . . literally . . . your shoes got
covered in pee. I peed all over your shoes. That's what this
is really about. I mean, they were drenched, I had so many
beers, and I had to pee so badly . . . I'm really sorry, like,
really, really sorry. I should have stopped peeing. I should
have taken your shoes off and just peed on my bare feet, that's
what a better person would have done, but I didn't think of it
at the time. I'm only thinking of that now, in fact.*

*I had a plan, though! When I fell in love with your Nikes
that morning, I was planning on ordering them that night for
myself anyway, and since we wear the same size, I thought,
"Okay, this is bad, Laura's shoes are covered in my pee, but
it's cool because I'll just order the new pair for her, and I'll
keep this pair with my pee on them. No biggie." Well, biggie.
That night I searched all over the World Wide Web, and
those navy Nikes were sold out everywhere. They were gone,
even on eBay. I feel terrible. I am really sorry. If it makes you
feel any better, I got really bad scrapes on one of my bum-
cheeks from the hedge I was squatting in front of. See, once I
saw what was happening, I rearranged my position, thinking*

that there was more of a slope downhill if I was bum to hedge instead of facing the hedge. It didn't really make much of a difference, though, and I just ended up getting several scrapes on the left half of my ass. When I got home, I hosed the shoes down and left them in the sun for a few hours, which my mother, a registered nurse, told me should kill all the odor and was safer than washing and risking ruining the shoes and then neither of us could have them. I'm sorry, Laura. I hope you can forgive me, you're not too mad, and you still want to be friends. I should have told you when I returned the shoes, but I just couldn't risk you refusing to lend me shoes again. You have such a great shoe wardrobe, and none of my other friends wear my size. I swear that I will only urinate in toilets while wearing your footwear from now on. I promise. I am the mayor of Promiseville. Just don't cut me off. I forget if you said you wear socks with those Nikes or not . . . I hope you said you did.

I Don't (Really) Have Enemies

RECENTLY, I WAS SITTING WITH LOMO (A.K.A. LAURA A. Moses) at a restaurant when a stranger walked past me. A woman. I didn't know her, but I was thinking of how happy I was that she didn't hate me. (Not that she necessarily liked me either, I have no idea, I'd never seen her before in my life.) I was writing this book at the time, and it got me thinking that I was really pleased knowing that I didn't have any enemies . . . that I know of. (Wait, does my friend's ex-husband who is a total douche bag count? I hate him, but I don't consider him an enemy per se, I just hate him.) I realized this also meant at no time would I ever be nervous to run into someone (except Matt Damon, but for starstruck reasons, not enemy reasons). I think this is because I don't lie to people anymore (unless someone asks if she looks fat and she does. I sometimes lie about that). I'm not patting myself on the back or anything, and I have lied plenty in the past (*plenty*), but in the last few years I realized that lying takes time and mental space and I just don't have either anymore. When you don't lie, among other things, you don't really have to ever fear running into anyone (except for Matt Damon, and I'm going to add my friend's ex-husband to this list too).

During my last foray into singledom, before I met my husband, I decided that I would date a lot instead of jumping into another relationship right away (even though I kind of jumped into a relationship with my husband right away). But I made a rule for myself: if I wasn't interested in going out with someone anymore, I was going to tell that person (unless there was some way I could get away with not telling that person—there never was). I wanted to do it for myself. I needed to learn to be more honest and direct (still need to learn that). I didn't want to text, or avoid people, or be nervous about the dreaded run-in (but I'm still nervous about running into Matt Damon, friend's ex-husband, and also my last therapist because I never officially quit therapy, I just quit going because I got really busy and had broken up with the guy I complained too much about during my sessions). For being one of the largest cities in the country, Los Angeles can be really small (except when you're driving in traffic, then it feels like the size of Asia). You are basically guaranteed to run into someone you don't want to, at some point, somewhere, when you least expect it. Most likely, when you didn't put makeup on, are hungover, leaving yoga and have crotch sweat (or just have regular non-yoga crotch sweat), and definitely when you have pinkeye and are buying a broom at a local hardware store (OK, in this instance it wasn't anyone I'd lied to, or who had lied to me, it was a famous actor I had worked with, but still, you get the point. And he was with his impossibly thin and gorgeous model girlfriend. You just always run into people at the worst times). Yep, that's when it will happen. But if you are always direct and honest with people, you really have nothing to fear. Except accidentally giving someone pinkeye (or a shark attack, or public speaking, change, an ear infection, car accident, mugging . . .).

So, if a guy I didn't really like called to ask me out again, I would say, "I had fun, but I don't want to go on dates with you anymore." (And, "You're really great and cute and special and awesome and I don't know what's wrong with me. It's me, not you. I'm such a jerk, you know what? Never mind. Let's keep dating.") There was usually a moment of silence, followed by a quick good-bye, and it was over, easy, just like that. (And sometimes the guys would say that they didn't want to go on dates anymore either and that's why they were calling, and I would cry, and then we would go out again.) I was given this wise but devastatingly simple advice by a male friend, and it really worked (I only did it twice). And I got good at it (again, only did it twice). And I have never been afraid to run into anyone ever again (except Matt Damon and friend's ex-husband, and last therapist, and people who have sent me scripts they have written that I haven't read yet). I didn't blow anyone off, I didn't lie or make up excuses, I just told the truth (twice). Actually, I think my friend Brad summed it up best when he recently said to me, "Judy, I'm not going to lie to you, sometimes I lie." (OK, Brad is kind of a friend; he is a prop master I have worked with twice. We'd probably be friends if we weren't so busy and . . .)

Random Judy Texts

SOME PEOPLE YOU HAVE TO TAKE TIME TO GET TO know; some people you just know. Janet and I are that kind of friends, the instant kind. We met our first days of college, and we have been sharing a brain, her dad's Levi's, and a thrifted gold cardigan ever since. Well, if I'm being honest, I can't fit in the Levi's anymore, she can, though, and that's the only thing I don't like about her. After sending in her description of what it was like to be friends with me (see chapter titled "The Ultimate Best Friend"), Janet decided to compile this list of all the random text messages I have sent to her over the past year. All but three of them are apropos of absolutely nothing. I guess I have been using my best friend as Twitter for as long as I can remember, because isn't this what Twitter is? When my publicist was trying to explain to me what to tweet about, she should have just said to tweet what I text to Janet every day. So I guess what I'm wondering is, is Twitter taking the place of our best friends? I don't want it to. I want Janet to get my thoughts as I think them, not tens of thousands of strangers. Yes, they can have them eventually, but I want an actual eye roll. I need it. I want a real person who loves me to tell me that I am ridiculous, because I need to hear it.

RANDOM JUDY TEXTS

For dinner I had 20oz of coffee and 5 Kraft singles. Am I going to die?

* * *

I am about to use my food processor for the first time in my life that I can remember.

* * *

#fuckyes! #welcomehome #thesunwillcomeoutnow #ionlyspeakinhashtagnow

* * *

Just cried during a Rust-Oleum commercial.

* * *

MY MOTHER IS DRIVING ME CRAZY!!!!!!

* * *

New Verizon iPhone commercial just made me cry. I'm at an airport. Humiliated.

* * *

$23 worth of Taco Bell and 3 hours later, back to our regular programming.

* * *

Lizard in bedroom. I repeat—lizard in bedroom. Did you hear me screaming? You did.

* * *

I am pooped. And I think I peed my pants a little. Should I be worried? Is that an old person thing?

* * *

Dude. I'm all for ghetto. Go ghetto or go home. That's like my main saying.

* * *

How old are we? No really. How old are we?

* * *

I've decided I really want a tee pee.

* * *

The woman behind me complained quite a bit about her UTI before the plane took off, and every time she went to the restroom, she grabbed my seat and pulled my hair. But don't feel bad for her, she's on antibiotics and it should clear up in a few days.

* * *

I just cried when I saw the poster for The Blindside.

* * *

I'm on a steady diet of Subway, red wine and NyQuil.

* * *

Beyonce. Is. Everything. I don't even know about Jason Bourne anymore.

* * *

PS I cried in yoga today when the teacher said the Baskin-Robbins closed.

* * *

They let celebrities high dive?

* * *

Don't get killed or die. OK? Promise?

* * *

The only thing worse than crying uncontrollably while watching a Tina Fey movie on an airplane is doing it while sitting next to two 16 year old boys. #newlow

* * *

Did I tell you my MOM gave me a breast exam last time she visited? Yeah, I made the mistake of telling my mom I thought I felt a lump. DON'T EVER DO THAT.

* * *

Sent from my iPhone

He Doesn't Have AIDS

I REMEMBER SO CLEARLY THE CONVERSATION WHEN Dean Johnsen told me he had kids. We were set up on a blind date by our mutual friend Matt but couldn't schedule it for a few weeks (because of his custody schedule, though I didn't know that at the time), so we just started talking on the phone. A lot. We talked on the phone almost every day before we even met. It was fun and romantic, and I liked feeling free to just talk without being self-conscious that my bangs were greasy, if I spilled sauce on my white shirt, or if I had a booger. It was a very stress-free way to get to know someone. Maybe that's what it's like to Internet date. Although I did like the idea that if this Dean Johnsen turned out to be a super jerk, I could punch Matt in the arm, and I would never be able to punch my computer in the arm for a bad fix up, and I knew I'd want to punish someone, not some thing— it's much more gratifying.

Dean didn't tell me about the kids or even the divorce for our first few phone dates, and then one night, a few days before our first actual in-person date, he said, "Did Matt tell you about me?" Immediately, my mind went to AIDS. He has AIDS. You see, my house is off what I lovingly refer to as AIDS Boulevard. It's not a boulevard of AIDS but a very busy road that is plastered with billboards touting the dangers of unsafe sex. It's a scary drive to the valley from my house, and since I was single again, I couldn't help but harbor a fear that I would end up like Molly Ringwald in the Lifetime movie where she got AIDS from sleeping with some bartender one time. Look, those billboards for safe sex work on me: they really freak me out! So, there I am, talking on the phone with my future husband, and he asks me a question like that? Of course I thought he had HIV, and of course I would get fixed up with a really nice, smart, funny guy who also had no immune system. Well, you can probably guess that he didn't have it (and doesn't, and neither do I. PSA: Have you been tested in a while? Should you? Yes), but he did tell me that he was divorced. That's it? Divorced? No big deal. I knew he was older than I was, and I wanted to date someone older since the Peter Pans of Los Angeles had yet to work out for me, and I figured an older man had the likelihood of being divorced. Then he told me he had kids . . . and that was OK too. I was sort of prepared for that possibility. I mean, you almost want an older guy to be divorced because if he's not, there could be a weird reason he never married. And if he is divorced, then chances are good he has kids. I admittedly didn't think it that far through at the time, but I wasn't shocked or even surprised.

The last bomb Dean dropped was that he lived in Thousand Oaks, California. That may mean nothing to a lot of you, but it is an hour away from where I live. And an hour and a half in L.A. traffic. At first I was silent on the phone, processing. I asked Dean about the Target that was there, right off the 101 highway. He said, "Yeah, we have a Target out here, but the one you're thinking of is in Woodland Hills. Thousand Oaks is farther than that." There was somewhere farther than that? I *was* thinking he meant Woodland Hills, which is still far, but about twenty minutes closer than the suburb he was talking about. Woodland Hills I could stomach. But then he told me Thousand Oaks was actually in Ventura County. There was a different area code for this land he lived in. Now I'm really spinning/reeling/freaking out. I realize I hadn't even gone on my first date with this guy, I still had no idea what he looked like, but still, I had to wonder how I would manage a relationship with anyone who lived in a different county than me. Until that point, I had a strict rule about not dating anyone on the Westside of Los Angeles, but this wasn't anything I'd even considered before. Divorce? Whatever. Kids? OK, fine. But an hour-plus commute if everything went the way I was hoping it would go? That was a tougher pill to swallow . . . an hour? And the kids live there? And so does their mom? And their grandma? And they all like it there? Do they have a lot of friends? What I'm getting at is that I was hoping that these young Johnsens had wanderlust and no friends or ties to the community and would love nothing more than to move with their dad to Los Angeles! Yes, my brain was moving way faster than our relationship was, but I *really* liked this Dean Johnsen, he gave good phone, and we'd already had the STD talk. Well, my fantasy was just that, a fantasy. His kids have all the friends. In fact, they seem to know almost everyone in that town. They play all the sports. They go to a public school, and it's a really good one, and since their mom and grandma also live there, they are not going anywhere.

Well, lucky for me, I was reading a book in my book club that made my decision to go through with the date an easy one. It was called *Marry Him* by Lori Gottlieb. Someone in my book club knew the author, I think, so we were reading it in hardcover. It was about how single women limit themselves with all their deal breakers when dating. I thought it was a little harsh, but Ms. Gottlieb made some good points, and I thought she might be right. Most of my single friends *did* seem to be limiting themselves by their prerequisites, and I felt maybe I was in danger of limiting myself as well. So, with this theme fresh in my head, I was willing to give this guy a shot. I had been striking out with guys my age who were geographically desirable, so why not go out with a guy who I knew owned a house and a car, had insurance, and made me laugh? Those items were high on the list I carried around in my wallet of what I wanted in a husband.

So, we finally had our first date. I was dying to see what this guy looked like. If he was as cute as he was funny, I was going to have a hard decision ahead of me. And he was. I liked him. A lot. I didn't meet his kids until we were serious, though. My first "date" with the kids was at Claim Jumper (their turf). But we sat in the bar (my turf). I brought them cupcakes as per my aunt Teresa's suggestion to win them over with sugar. Things went really well, and eventually we started having sleepovers in Thousand Oaks even on nights he had the kids. Judge if you must, but we waited until we were super in love, and the kids seemed to like having me and Buckley around.

And I can't leave out their mother, the Sheriff. For a really long time my friends thought I was joking and that was a nickname I made up for her, but no. She is an actual sheriff in Ventura County. I feel like a character Paul Rudd would play in a romantic comedy about a guy who finds out the gal he likes has an ex who's a cop. But it's not Paul Rudd, it's me, and it's not a movie, it's my life. My competition is Sheriff Barbie. Oh, yeah, did I mention the Sheriff is hot? She has a rockin' body and long blond hair and is, miraculously, always tan. And she carries a gun, everywhere. When she runs to the bathroom during one of Emilee's soccer games and asks me to keep an eye on her purse, I have to think twice about whether or not I want that kind of responsibility. She is nice, though, and fun, and we get along really well. I am super lucky. I'll take gun-toting police Barbie over a bat-shit-crazy ex who hates my guts and makes it her mission in life to make me miserable. Yeah, I got it good, because I have heard horror stories, like scarier than the *Saw* movies.

Our relationship was picking up pace, and I started spending more and more time in TO (Thousand Oaks). I was getting used to the suburban atmosphere. It reminded me of the Southern California version of where I grew up, yet so different from everywhere I'd lived since. I loved that there wasn't much traffic, there was ample parking, well-stocked chain stores were everywhere, and it was safe—thanks in part to the Sheriff. People's lives seemed to revolve around their kids and the community. No one had a nanny, and families ate dinner together every night. Dean told me it was like Mayberry, and after looking up what that was, I have to agree. I especially liked that Hollywood wasn't a player in this town, and no one cared what I did for a living.

Soon we got engaged and started to talk about where we were going to live. Dean's job is a five-minute drive from my house in Hollywood, and he only has the kids half of the time; it didn't really make sense for him to have that commute every single day if he didn't *have* to. Dean had been driving three hours a day for years, his back hurt, he had 200,000 miles on his hybrid, and I had a perfectly good house that we could stay in on the days we didn't have the kids. And selfishly, I was nervous about being out there alone during the days that Emilee and Lucas were with their mom. I thought the transition would be easier for me if I got to hang on to a little bit of my old life. So we decided to change nothing. We never moved in with each other. And as of today, we still haven't. "If it ain't broke, don't fix it," my dad has told me a million times. So we didn't. We lead a very double life. Or we have the best of both worlds, depending on your preferred idiom.

Dean and I fell in love and got married, and I became a stepmom in a faraway land (fifty-three miles from my house, to be exact). In the deal I got two kids, a crazy long commute every other week, an ex-wife, and another dog! Most people just get a new set of dishes. It's been fun, and half of the time we have a totally newlywed-like lifestyle. We go out to eat, see bands play, get drinks a lot, see movies, hang out with friends. And the other half of the time we hang out at the local baseball field, carpool to and from soccer practice, try to think of fun things to do as a family between sports, and then collapse into bed, totally exhausted, wondering how we will make it to Friday, kind of like every other family in the world. But it's awesome! In the beginning, I didn't have a clue. I didn't know where anything was in that town. I got lost driving home from a drop-off two blocks away. I couldn't remember the days we had the kids and the days we didn't. It was a gigantic change for me, but I think I'm kind of getting the hang of it, or at least I'm getting better at hiding the fact that I'm not.

Best Advice
I've Ever Gotten

I LOVE ADVICE. I LOVE ENCOURAGING WORDS, AND my bookshelves reflect this. But I am also pretty certain that most people know more than I do about almost everything. I think I can come off at times as a bit of a know-it-all, but it's really just a defense mechanism I have cultivated after years of feeling like a total imbecile. I do love learning from others, though, and I want the real experts (about everything!) to teach me. This idea was the basis for my Web series, *Reluctantly Healthy*. It was really just an excuse for me to gather expert advice and share it with the world for free! Instead of paying a trainer or chef or nutrition-ist to tell me what to do, I can just have a few cameras film the whole session, air it on Yahoo!, and I'm set! Advice for me and the masses! I think I really nailed that one.

Of course sometimes there is advice that no one can help me with. There are just some life lessons that we all have to learn on our own, and those are the hardest. There aren't a lot of quotes and advice I live by—I forget them too easily, unless I write them on Post-its all over my kitchen—but these have done me pretty well thus far. And in the interest of sharing the *Reluctantly Healthy* way (minus the cameras and airing it on the Internet), I thought I'd pass them along to you, too.

"When in doubt, sing loud."
— MRS. HUTCHINSON, CHOIR TEACHER, HIGH SCHOOL

She was being literal when she said this to me my junior year, I did it, and I got a solo in *The Pajama Game* that I should *not* have gotten because my singing voice is challenged, at best. My co-star had to hum the tune in my ear during the performance, which I later learned was picked up on the mic. But whatever! She was right. I've heard "Go big, or go home," but I like Mrs. H.'s version better. Also, because it reminds me of my audition and how when I left the room that afternoon someone in the hallway said, "Oh my God, that sound was you singing?"

"Don't shit where you eat."
— MOMS EVERYWHERE

I remember it first coming out of my mom's mouth when I left for college but have heard it since a lot, and it's 100 percent right. It ruins everything. I have written this on *a lot* of Post-it notes, in addition to several times in this book already.

"Don't pluck your eyebrows when you're drunk."
— BEST FRIEND JANET

She yelled this at me over the phone the morning after I got drunk in college and couldn't find my eyebrows on my face. OK mornings after.

"Take arnica for a few weeks before getting any cosmetic procedures done."

—ANONYMOUS

I actually have no memory of who told me this, but it works . . . I hear . . . not that I would know . . . I mean, you know, it's just the word on the street . . . from people who have had stuff done . . . not me . . .

"If you're in bed, and you think you might have to pee, just get up and pee. You won't stop thinking about it until you do. Just get up and pee already."

—ME, EVERY MORNING AND OFTEN IN THE MIDDLE OF THE NIGHT

Oh, the hours of sweet sleep I will never get back because I lay there just trying to convince myself I could wait until my alarm went off to go to the bathroom.

"If you're a girl, pee after sex."

—AWESOME NURSE PRACTITIONER FROM MY LOCAL PLANNED PARENTHOOD IN COLLEGE

This anecdote has been censored for the sake of my stepchildren and my dignity. But I would like to take this opportunity to thank that Planned Parenthood nurse. She was awesome and probably saved a lot of lives in Chicago. Hopefully, she still is!

"Pack half of what you think you need."

—LAURA A. MOSES, FRIEND, EXPERT PACKER, AND CONSTANT TRAVELER

"You get more bees with honey."

—LUCILLE SELIG, BUSINESS MANAGER

She is awesome, another parent to me here in this big city, and the reason I have good credit and a retirement account and my phone never got shut off.

"Wear your underwear over your tights; it will keep them from sagging."

—MOM

This is *not* the best advice I've ever gotten—it's not "follow your dreams" or "only compare you to you," and if you're planning on having a make-out session with a fellow waiter after work when you're nineteen and you think that kissing *might* lead to his hand reaching up your skirt and feeling a pair of full-bottom panties over your tights, don't do it. He will get totally weirded out, and there is no amount of explaining that will ever make him look at you the same again. Not that this ever happened to me, no way, I just have a really vivid imagination. But otherwise, my mom's right, it really does keep your tights from sagging.

"The best time to plant an apple orchard is twenty years ago; the second best time is today."

—DOUG CHALKE VIA SARAH CHALKE

She said this to me and Marla Sokoloff at one of our lunches when I was being a whiny baby about all the bad decisions I had made in the past. She's right. For example, yes, it would have been great if I would have broken up with what's-his-name three years ago, ideally moments after becoming his girlfriend, but I still did it, and that's what counts today.

"Nice and easy does it."

— FRANK SINATRA VIA JEFFREY TAMBOR

I took acting class when I got to L.A. with Jeffrey Tambor. In one class he played us that song by Frank Sinatra and told us to think of acting that way. Don't stress, don't push, don't act hard, just do it nice and easy. I think it works for a lot more than acting.

"Crazy things happen to crazy people."

— DAVID GARDNER, BEST MANAGER EVER

This is not necessarily advice, but in my mind it applies. You know that crazy person in your life? Friend, family member, in-law, whatever, who always has crazy things happen to him or her? And you're always like, "What? Again? How can this much weird shit happen to this one person?" That's why. Don't waste your (my) time trying to figure it out.

"Always wash your face before bed."

— EVERY FASHION MAGAZINE EVER AND JANET

I want to make this my number one piece of advice, but that would make me seem shallow. I'd also like to add that this is a good barometer for how drunk you were the night before, if you washed your face or not before bed, but that would make me seem like a lush.

"Don't engage the creature."

— DEAN JOHNSEN, HUSBAND

If someone is a wild card, best to just leave him or her be. I've told this to a lot of people regarding breakups and responding to/initiating e-mails/texts/calls.

"Never promise crazy a baby."

—GEORGE BLUTH SR., REGARDING PROMISING KITTY SANCHEZ
A BABY WHILE HIDING OUT IN MEXICO WITH HER

This isn't advice that was given to me personally, but a favorite quote of mine from *Arrested Development*. But I'm sure it applies to someone somewhere.

"Walk around the house like a fucking champion."

—PINTEREST

Correction: I think *this* should always be my number one piece of advice.

All-Time Lonely

I THINK 2012 WAS MY ALL-TIME LONELY. WHICH IS ironic because it started out as my all-time happy. I had just gotten married, I had a string of great jobs, and the people around me were healthy and doing well. Maybe that's why. Maybe I was finally so happy with my life and the people in it that I didn't want to leave it anymore, for the first time I wasn't looking for anything different, I didn't want a change, I liked what I had. Before I met my husband, I always jumped at the chance to work far away. I thought I would find what I was looking for somewhere else, some great discovery that would give my life meaning and change me for the better. It was my favorite thing to do. I wanted to do it more often. I would jump at the chance to leave town and reinvent myself for a month.

It's different now. I have a harder time away. Now I'm married, I am in love. I have stepkids, and even though I know they don't need me, I need them. I miss home. I miss my dog. I miss sleeping next to Dean Johnsen. It took me so long to find him, and I hate every day we're not together making up for lost time. Now work really feels like work. My friends with small children always tell me to cherish the time alone, and do I know what they would give for even a few days alone somewhere? Yes, I do, because that's what I would give to be home with my family. I know the grass is always greener, so I try to enjoy it, but it's different now. These last few jobs have been particularly difficult. I knew that I was feeling pretty bad when I decided to get some fish while I was on a six-month job in New York. I was sick of being all alone in my little corporate rental apartment. I thought goldfish would be the perfect antidote. I could get two fat-bellied little fish that would hang out in a round bowl on my kitchen table and keep me company while I ate and worked on my lines. I would name one Michael Dorsey, after Dustin Hoffman's character in *Tootsie*, and the other Dorothy Michaels, after the character Michael Dorsey played in *Tootsie*. (I've always had a fantasy of finally seeing them together, even if in fish form. You know if *Tootsie* was made now, it would totally be a Tyler Perry movie.) I went to the pet store and asked the man to help set me up with everything I would need. Well, the pet store man was not on board with my plan. It might have been my fault. I was trying not to cry, so I was brief with my words and staring up at the lights in the ceiling a lot (that works by the way, if you don't want to cry). He basically told me he wouldn't sell me two goldfish. He told me they were stinky and that I would have to change the water every single day. He asked me how large my apartment was because if it was small, Michael and Dorothy were sure to overwhelm the place with fish stink. I remembered years ago checking out a one-bedroom sublet on the Lower East Side that had a turtle in it, and that apartment did smell like turtle. I hated that the pet store man was right. He told me I should get a betta fish. One betta fish. Well, I didn't want *one* betta fish. They're mean and they kill their own if you put them together; it's a bloodbath, I've heard. He wanted to set me up with a whole betta fish system. They sold them in kits. It was a tank you plugged into the wall, and it had a motor and a filter and everything. This was not my plan. What happened to the days when you could throw a couple of goldfish in a bowl and feed them every day? Is that not a thing anymore? The fact that the betta fish have to be alone in their tanks, that I couldn't get two, made me feel even lonelier. Now me *and* the fish would be on our own? I'll admit that I was suffering from PMS and my mind was starting to spiral, but I couldn't help but think, what if I was like a betta fish, and I can't be in a tank with another fish because I will kill it? Is that why I get so many jobs out of town? Is the universe trying to tell me something? I left the pet store empty-handed and feeling worse.

A few days later I took the train to Boston from New York to spend the night with my friends Scott and Jojo, who had just moved there from L.A. They had nothing in their apartment yet except two beds and two cats. I am allergic to cats, but when Jojo told me that the baby cat, Larry, might sleep with me if I lured him into my bed with some sliced turkey meat, I got so excited I took a precautionary Benadryl. I was starved for something real and furry to cuddle with. That night I got all ready for bed and got my turkey plate ready. I gave him a few pieces in the kitchen and walked with the turkey into the bedroom. He didn't follow me as I had hoped. I could sense that he was lurking in the hallway but not ready to come into the room yet. I pretended to be really engrossed in an infomercial about an airbrush makeup kit (backfired because now I need it, obviously) in an attempt to play hard to get with the cat. Unfortunately, I overdid it with the playing hard to get and fell asleep. When I woke up in the morning, the first thing I saw when I opened my eyes was the plate of turkey, untouched, on the pillow next to mine. This is my all-time lonely. Trying to lure a cat that I'm allergic to into snuggling with me by leaving a plate of deli turkey meat next to my head. At breakfast that morning Jojo told me their other cat, Steven, only likes fresh turkey slices, or he might have come in. But since the meat was a few days old, I was stuck with Larry. Great. So not only was I sleeping with deli meat, but it was several-days-old deli meat. Larry's an asshole. I think I'm going to try for a plant next time, or possibly a Roomba.

How to Feed
Your Stepchildren

THIS IS HOW I THINK I CAN BEST DESCRIBE WHAT IT'S like to be a new stepparent: Have you ever spent the weekend at a friend's house who has kids? You know how you wake up in the morning and wander into the kitchen in your houseguest jammies and walk directly to the coffeepot and pour yourself a hot cup of coffee and then ask your host if there's anything you can do to help? You don't really mean it, because you don't know what to do or where anything is, but you offer because it's the polite thing to do. Your host says no, but thanks. You wander with your hot steamy cup of coffee to the bathroom, and take a long, hot shower, and get ready for your day.

Well, take that memory, but now the host is a tall, hot guy, and instead of saying, "No, but thanks," he kisses you and says, "YES! Could you make a turkey sandwich for Lucas, a lunch for Emilee, she likes peanut butter and jelly, maybe start some scrambled eggs and bagels for breakfast, I'm going to hop in the shower real quick, oh, and if the exterminator calls, can you talk to him and see if he can come at noon on Monday, but if he can't, ask him what days he's free, and then we'll figure it out. Oh, and did you decide what you wanted to do about that broken dresser? Do you want me to call the place and see if they will switch it out, or should we just try to fix it? What should we have for dinner tonight? I can make turkey burgers again, if that's easy? Oh, wait, you're not eating meat right now, shit, OK, well, let's talk about it on the phone while I drive to work. I have to get in the shower, I love your ass big-time!!" And then you spill blazing-hot coffee all over the front of your new, kid-friendly jammies when you lean in for your express kiss. That's what it's like.

As an adult, I always had a hard time imagining my future with any real clarity. It was always vague, nothing concrete. There were assumptions—I assumed I would get married, I assumed I would have kids, a job, a house, friends, and be moderately healthy. Yet I didn't know where, how many, what, or who. There was one specific, ongoing fantasy that involved Matt Damon, traveling the world, having long straight hair, and being able to speak French, but who doesn't fantasize about Matt Damon? I never imagined I would marry someone with kids, but I never imagined I wouldn't either. I just had no position on it either way. Lucky for me, Dean Johnsen's kids are awesome and easy and seemed to like me well enough, plus, he's nice (and hot), so I dove into the deep end, even though I've never been a strong swimmer.

I'm a perfectionist by nature, so naturally I wanted to be the perfect stepparent. The only problem was I had no clue what I was doing or what I was supposed to be doing. I couldn't even find any books on the topic (turns out I didn't look hard enough; there are thousands), but with reckless abandon I was ready for my new life! My therapist at the time warned me that it could be a real challenge, that I would have all the responsibility but without any of the authority. This is a catchphrase I find myself using a lot at parties when describing what my role is, but I'm not sure

I believe it anymore. Did it mean that I can't let them set something on fire, but then not discipline them if they try? I wasn't sure what the challenges were that I could look forward to, but at the time I believed "what does not kill us makes us stronger," and as long as his offspring didn't literally kill me, I would manage. (I would like to add here that I no longer subscribe to that philosophy. I think it's a lie, and I've thrown out all my inspirational artwork that states it.)

I was thrilled that his kids were older—nine (Lucas) and thirteen (Emilee)—so I wouldn't have to change their diapers, make sure they didn't cut my dog with scissors, or keep them from beating the shit out of each other. They were already too far along in school for me to be able to help with homework, so with that out of the way it would be easy, right? They had their own lives; I just needed to be around to feed and drive them. And, in the beginning, those were the biggest hurdles. I was a bad driver and an inexperienced cook. I didn't know where anything was located where they lived, and neither did they. Early on, I volunteered to drive Lucas to his friend's house, and we got in the car, I started it and said, "OK! So, where is Kyle's house?" and Lucas shrugged and said, "I don't know." Well, duh, of course he didn't know. He was nine. Nine-year-olds don't know where stuff is. They don't have addresses in the contacts of their phones; they don't enter all their playdates in their iCal. Amateurs.

I remembered how afraid I was of middle school and high school students when I was in middle school and high school. Kids in general freak me out. I have a terrible sailor's mouth (no one told me "crap" was a swear word!), I had no idea what they did in school all day, so I couldn't ask them about it, and I'd never turned on a Disney movie or kid channel in my life. I can't bear the TV shows on those kid networks, and I found myself getting really judgy about the acting and story lines. I wanted my "steps" to have better taste than that. I learned to stomach *Good Luck Charlie* because I had worked with the dad on that show, Eric Allan Kramer, and he was cool; *SpongeBob SquarePants* because it was so weird; and *iCarly* for I don't know why, it was just always on and I started to get sucked in, that Miranda Cosgrove is really charismatic. I didn't understand why they didn't like what I liked, since the stuff I liked was so cool! Also, and no offense to kids in general, but for the most part they are terrible conversationalists. You ask them about their day, they say either fine, nothing, cool, or OK. Actually, if you ask them about anything, they say it is fine/nothing/cool/OK. And if I'm being really honest, I was scared of them. And I think they knew it; I think they could smell it on me. I hadn't been around that many kids, I was inexperienced, and I was terrified they could sense it and use my weaknesses for evil as I would have at their age.

I ordered SiriusXM for my car so I could start listening to parenting channels during my ninety-minute commute. Oprah had a great program that was really helpful. The psychologist lady during one show said that what you were supposed to do was just "be" around your kids. So I would ask my steps the regular questions, I would get the regular answers, and then I tried to just "be," but I started to feel boring. I would find myself staring off into space a lot. Playing with my phone, telling them about my day, and realizing that they don't care at all. I was really excited to get some professional insight on these talk shows, but I always seemed to arrive at my destination just as the host/guest would say, "And here is the ultimate thing you should do, Judy, to make them love you and be the greatest stepparent in the world . . ." OK, I am exaggerating, but it was sort of like that. I always missed the summary, or the answer to the call-in question that was my exact same question!! It was always, "We'll be back after this break with the answer to that amazing question! Don't go anywhere!" FUCK YOU, RADIO HOST! I AM IDLING IN A PARKING SPACE AND LATE FOR A MEETING, I NEED THE ANSWER NOW!!!! When are they going to invent DVR for radios? Yes, I know I could probably listen on my laptop, but when? I can't have it playing while I cook, because I need total concentration in order not to ruin every meal completely, and I can't play the shows while I'm cleaning, because I don't want anyone to hear my tricks and learn my secret—that I have no idea what I'm doing and I'm scared and don't want to mess it all up. I finally gave up and went back to listening to music or Doctor Radio, another commuter obsession of mine. I may not be getting parenting tips anymore, but I love hearing doctors break down diseases like takotsubo cardiomyopathy and pica.

In the beginning, the hands-down, 100 percent hardest thing about being a new stepmom was feeding my new stepchildren. I am kind of getting it down now, three years in, but it had been my greatest struggle, my greatest fear, and my greatest use of swear words. It is hard to feed kids who are not your own and who you have never spent any time with until now, when you suddenly spend all your time with them. The hardship is compounded when you've only ever fed yourself for your entire adult life, and barely even that. I don't want to throw my kids under the bus, because they are so awesome, and they are trying hard to eat my food, but they were hard to feed. Or easy, depending on how you look at it. Easy, if I only fed them the beige food they loved best. Hard, if I wanted them to eat green food, or anything that was mixed together or from a foreign country. They didn't like fruit. No veggies. No casseroles (a midwestern staple), no lasagna, we could swing a taco night, but nothing more foreign than that. And no leftovers, not even Halloween candy. I'm not kidding. If the Halloween candy wasn't eaten days after Halloween, it would sit in the pantry, uneaten, until I would have to throw it out so I didn't binge. It mystified me. But that is not my only food-related problem. My second-biggest problem was remembering to feed them. It would completely slip my mind because I was just used to myself. I need to eat when I am hungry, but I can also wait. I can grab some nuts and a banana to tide me over, or even substitute that for a meal if I get wrapped up in whatever else I'm doing. This is a no-no with kids. You have to feed them meals, the main ones. And they get hungry after school, before soccer/baseball/basketball practice, and when they get home from practice, they are starving and literally about to pass out in the kitchen while I scramble to put something together that is hot and not a turkey sandwich, which I already made them for lunch. It was all new to me, and it was hard. Food has taken on a new meaning for me now that I have steps. It is now a necessity. It is a major part of my thinking all day, every day, and on the weekends, planning for the week ahead. Food is not for enjoying anymore or to experiment with. It needs to be a fastball down the middle (a baseball reference I have picked up since spending countless hours at Little League). It is for fuel, for health, and mostly to stop them from banging the cabinet doors open and closed at 10:00 p.m. while I am concentrating on Pinterest and wine. If they're still hungry at 10:00 p.m., I feel like a failure. I feel like the worst stepparent and American in the history of stepparents and Americans when I am throwing food in the garbage because I know they won't eat it if it's left over. Also, when you're used to cooking for only yourself and the occasional dinner for two (and I mean *occasional*), it seems impossible to cook a meal for four people. I don't even have a clue about how much food to buy. I don't know if I'm supposed to double recipes or if they are already written with four hungry people in mind. What about supermarkets? I never pushed a cart in them; I only ever needed a basket. I was basket-at-market girl, not cart-pusher girl. I had no idea where anything was in the market. It would take me hours to shop—I still take forever, but I am starting to shave seconds off my time. In the beginning I would lose myself in the store, looking for one special thing in the recipe, not realizing that (a) I could make it without and (b) no one was going to want to eat what I made anyway. Then I started the phase where I let Dean Johnsen cook for the kids, and I made a healthy meal for the two of us. That worked for a while, but it didn't really solve the meta-problem of getting the kids to eat healthier and expand their palates to include more exotic foods. It made me laugh when my friends would say, "Just put some avocado and sprouts on a piece of toast." Uh, yeah, that's not happening. It's a process, and it's getting better, but there's a ways to go yet. I'm getting better at cooking meals for all of us, at not taking it personally when they hate something or don't want to eat it, at not wanting to cry when Lucas puts a bite of food the size of his pinkie nail on his fork and examines it for seventeen seconds before putting it in his mouth. Lucas, if you read this, I *promise* I am not trying to poison you. (Speaking of poison, I do think it's a small miracle the four of us haven't had food poisoning from any of my meals yet. Knocking on wood right now.)

Another major adjustment I had to make was learning to deal with the highs and lows surrounding sports. Well, actually, the adjustment started with just attending sports. Besides hockey games with my dad when I was little, I hadn't really attended any sport competitions that didn't involve a guy also taking me to dinner before and drinks after. This was way different. The first time I went to one of Lucas's Little League games was a really intense experience. Dean and I had only been dating for a few months. I had already met the kids, and it wasn't Dean's weekend with them, so we were going to go away to Santa Barbara. But we just had to make one stop on the way to watch Lucas's game. It was a championship game (which meant nothing to me at the time) against the rival team (again, meant nothing to me then). To add more fun (read: pressure) to the afternoon, I was meeting Dean's mom (also named Judy) *and* ex-wife for the first time. Dean had told me that no one really took the games that seriously, it didn't matter who won or lost, it was all about the kids having fun, getting out in the sunshine, and getting some exercise. Liar. Lucas's team lost, all the kids were crying, and the coach of the opposing team donned a court jester hat and was prancing around the baseball diamond cheering and screaming. Lucas was clutching his dad around the waist, trying to hide his tears. I waited with the ex-wife, Dean's mom, and Emilee a ways away. Dean finally talked Lucas into feeling a little less suicidal and then came jogging over to me, all smiles until we got in the car and he said, "Ready to go get drunk and have sex in Santa Barbara?!" I was in shock. Is this how it is all the time? Is this how all the coaches are? Is it going to be this dramatic and intense forever? Was this Dean's version of "not taking the games seriously"? I didn't know how to process it. I didn't know how I was going to handle Little League. I was going to need a lot more wine and a prescription for Xanax.

I had a similar experience with Emilee but much later, after I was already official. She had a soccer tournament in gorgeous Lancaster, California, on the same day Lucas had a baseball game near home, so I offered to drive and attend Emilee's game so Dean could stay with Lucas, divide and conquer, a term I have become very familiar with. Lancaster is about a two-hour drive into the desert. It's a wonderful place if you need to hide out or buy some meth. About forty-five minutes into our drive out there, my tire exploded on the freeway. I swore (oops), pulled over, called AAA, and told Emilee to text her friend and teammate Gabby. Knowing that Gabby is always late to everything, I was confident that they hadn't passed us yet and would be a few minutes behind us. They were. Gabby's dad pulled over, grabbed Em, and left

Gabby's mom to wait with me for the AAA man to ensure that I didn't get raped or bitten by a snake and so the girls could get to their game on time. Everything worked out fine, the AAA guy put my spare on, from Lucas's baseball game Dean called a tire store in Lancaster and made an appointment for me to buy a new tire after the game, and Em was going to hitch a ride home with a teammate so she didn't have to spend one more second than necessary in Lancaster. Well, the game turned into a disaster. We were neck and neck but at the last minute lost, and Emilee, who was playing defense, thought the winning goal scored was her fault. She cried and didn't want to ride home with any of the other players because she felt she had let them down. It was the first time I had ever seen her feel anything but two emotions—unreadable and vaguely content. And now she was crying next to me in the lobby of America's Tire. I didn't know what to do or how to make her feel better, so I kept quiet, took her to Subway, and let her pick the music for the ride home. I have since seen her cry one other time, at another soccer game defeat, in a different methy desert town. There is something about the combination of me/Emilee/soccer/desert that is bad luck. Luckily, that time it wasn't her fault they lost, and she had headphones for the drive home, so we could both avoid an uncomfortable silence or worse, me trying lamely to comfort her while pushing my Prius to accelerate beyond sixty miles an hour.

I really think I could write an entire book about my experiences as a stepmother. I tried to make a TV show about it. Dean Johnsen gave me the thumbs-up when we got engaged to sell the idea to ABC, because it was a pretty wild story. L.A. actress meets the man of her dreams who lives fifty miles outside the city with his two kids, his ex-wife is a sheriff, lives with the sergeant, and Dean's mom, with the same name as me, lives a few blocks away. I remember when I would pitch my story, people would laugh and think I was lying, but I wasn't. I'm not. It's real. I became a parent to two preteens, and their mom carries a gun and fights crime for a living. Oh, and I mentioned she's hot, right? Yeah.

I don't know what my advice would be for people entering into a mixed family. I have no idea what the hell I'm doing most of the time, but it's fine! Dean told me no one does, and I choose to believe him. Yes, there are challenges, but it's so specific to the people. My kids are amazing. They are smart, funny, kind, and attractive. My husband's ex-wife is all of those things too, and we get along so well, she's just scarier because of the crime fighting, and his mom doesn't drop by nearly as much as I wish she would, but it's working out. I didn't know how to relate to his kids when I started my journey as their new parent. We didn't listen to the same music, we didn't watch the same TV shows, we hadn't seen the same movies, we didn't like the same restaurants, but one thing we did have in common is that we all loved Dean Johnsen, and I think that's as good a place to start as any.

Merry KISSmas! Love, Dean, Emilee, Lucas, and Judy

Jobs I Could Have Instead of Being an Actor

I BELIEVE THAT EVERYONE IN THE WORLD HAS ONE Oscar-worthy performance in them, and I'm not just saying that because I want to win an Oscar someday. If you're perfectly cast as yourself, the material is great, and you have great co-stars and a great director, it could happen. What's hard about acting, besides getting that job with the great script, actors, and director, is the technical stuff. It's hard to look at a piece of tape instead of the actor you're talking to in a scene so your eyes are closer to the camera lens, to be soaking wet in a scene for ten hours, to be freezing cold but acting like you're burning hot, to wear shoes giving you terrible blisters, sometimes just talking and walking can be a challenge when there's a giant camera pointed at your face and countless silent strangers staring at you. It can be terrifying, like you got shot with a tranquilizer gun after doing seven espresso shots. It's weird. But saying words and meaning them is kind of easy, I think.

I have a hard time believing people when they say they could never do what I do. Personally, I think that it's way harder to do almost everything else out there. Yes, you have to be OK with talking in front of strangers, and being scrutinized, and the rejection, but there are occupational hazards in every job, in fact way more dangerous ones, and once you get used to it, and remind yourself that you don't have to wear a bulletproof vest to work every day (unless the role you're playing calls for one), it's not so hard. The real question becomes, can you ever get used to it? I am rejected five times as much as I'm hired, probably more, but I think it (mostly) gets easier. Except when I have PMS, then it's way worse.

Sometimes I do wish I could just have the same job every day; it seems comforting to me—to work with the same people all the time, know your salary every year, know when you can take a vacation and plan it. I think I could get used to that. A little stability would be so different, and I find myself daydreaming about it, especially now that I'm married and have stepkids. I want to plan a vacation with them and actually be able to go on it. I can tell you one of the easiest ways to book an acting job, though: plan a trip that is very costly and nonrefundable; that's a surefire way to get a great gig, works every time!

There are some jobs out there that I know I could never do at this point in my life. I could never scoop ice cream. It's so frozen and hard, and I always marvel when people get a perfect scoop on my cone. My ice cream scoops come out the size of a large almond. I could never work in a drive-thru at a fast-food restaurant. I think they are real heroes. How do they keep all those orders and numbers in their heads? I mean, they are taking one order, *and* getting out change for another, *and* handing a bag of food out the window, it seems impossible to me. Schoolteacher? Thank you and God bless you all, but I don't think I have what it takes to keep my cool while little kids are literally peeing their pants in front of me, not to mention keeping all the food allergies straight these days. Any kind of ass-kicking job is out, for obvious reasons, but also I am not really good in potentially life-threatening situations. I freeze in peril, and that is not what you want from your cop/firefighter/paramedic. So here is a short list of jobs that I could see myself being good at and maybe even thriving in.

MANICURIST—I have to admit this one is appealing. My mother was convinced that I should go to cosmetology school when I first moved to L.A. She thought it would be a good way to earn money while I tried to get acting work. After meeting several manicurists, I realized that was absurd, that I couldn't just manicure in my spare time. One girl worked at a fancy salon, and she hustled! She had to really develop her business and establish a client base, and it seemed exhausting, almost as exhausting as trying to get acting work. I did consider it for about three minutes a long time ago but then thought better of it, because I thought I should work that hard to make it as an actor. But still, I kind of have to agree with my mom a little, after seeing the movie *Children of a Lesser God* when I was younger, being a manicurist seemed like an awesome job, and I'm not ruling it out for the future. Pro: I get to sit down all day. Con: I'm terrible at drawing, and everyone wants nail art these days.

ACTING TEACHER—Self-explanatory. Although, if I'm being honest, I don't think I'm a big enough person to deal well with my students having more success than me. (*Yet*. I would get there.) And because of that, I would, no doubt, need to take all the credit for their success.

PERFUME SALESGIRL—Nothing against the gals (and guys) who do this, but I think I would excel at this job. I could stand there in a chic outfit and ask people to smell my perfume. And I could ask if they wanted a sample or tempt them with a gift set for that special someone. (Oh my stars! I just realized I wrote "my" perfume instead of just "perfume." Was that a Freudian slip? I do really want my own perfume, and if I had to be the one to spray it, in person, all over strangers, so be it! At least I would really believe in the product!)

TARGET TEAM MEMBER—I could most definitely have a job at my local Target. I know where everything is in that store. I know how to fold; I know how to arrange the hangers by size/color. I think I could do it all, except maybe heavy lifting at first—I'd have to work into that. Added benefit: I look good in red.

PERSONAL ASSISTANT—OK, I'm not just saying this because I have played so many characters that are personal assistants, but I really think I would be awesome at that job. I am really good at organizing, I have a decent memory, a decent sense of style (helps for packing and red-carpet prep, except for my own for some reason), I'm good at gift purchasing, I love animals, and I'm very trustworthy and could be discreet if I had to. My main hurdles would be answering phone calls, e-mails, and text messages. I am really bad at that in my own life, but perhaps I would be better for my boss, due to the fact that not being an actor would free up some time in my day.

ADVICE COLUMNIST—This is my most secret passion. I would *love* to have my own advice column, à la Ann Landers or Dear Abby. I have no real education to back up my advice except for hours and hours spent on the sofa in therapy and having had loads of dysfunctional friends (OK, mostly myself), and I don't think there is a self-help book I have not at least read the table of contents of. No, I have no formal education in advice giving, but I'm smart enough to know when I don't know something, and that's pretty good, right?

MAIL CARRIER IN LOS ANGELES—Yeah, it has to be L.A. I mean, the weather is just amazing, and the mail carriers here seem to have it figured out. I have had several, and all of them are so cool! One girl wore a tight mini-mail-skirt, a fitted button-down, giant gold hoop earrings, and Dr. Martens boots. I wanted to be her friend, she didn't. Another guy had a more laid-back version of his uniform with baggy pants, baggy shirt kind of half tucked in (very French!), and white earbuds. He was always rocking out to music and didn't pay attention to anyone but seemed really happy all the time. And my current mail lady is sporting a mail skort, a tailored but untucked short-sleeved mail shirt, a very chic asymmetrical red bob haircut, and yesterday I could have sworn a full row of fake lashes. She didn't smile when I said hi to her, but I hope to win her over around the holidays. I know why none of them say hi to me, my dogs bark a lot, yes, but the real reason is that seven years ago I bought myself a new mailbox but have yet to hang it up on the wall. So the mail carriers always have to bend down to the ground to deliver my mail. If/when I'm a mail carrier, I will be irritated by that too. Maybe we'll bond over it! I really need to hang that thing up, for her. Oh, and it's good exercise, and blue really brings out the color in my eyes.

One Is Not the Loneliest Number

I AM AN ONLY CHILD. MY PARENTS HAD ME, AND then, two years later, my mom got her tubes tied. That was a conscious decision. She told me that a year ago when I asked her why she and my dad didn't have more kids. I know I have asked her this before and I don't remember her answers, but this time she was honest with me, which is why it stood out. It wasn't like she tried again and couldn't; they didn't want any more kids. My parents were done. They loved me and seemed to like being parents to me, but they didn't want their life to change any more than it already had, so they decided to quit while they were ahead.

As I'm sure any other only child has experienced, people are always asking me what it was like to be an only child. But I don't know how to answer that question. What is it like to be a girl? Or a boy? What is it like to breathe? I don't know anything different. I just know what my life was like, but I don't know what it was like compared with anything else. I've met loads of people who have siblings—in fact most of the people I know have brothers and sisters—and I don't ask them all the time what it was like, because I know they'd say, "I don't know. What was it like to be an only child?" and we're exactly where we started. People also tell me I don't seem like an only child. I think it's meant as a compliment, but what does that mean? I haven't met loads of asshole only children. If you fill a room with all the assholes you know, I'd bet that most of them have siblings. How many people am I being compared with? Maybe we've gotten a bad reputation, but I don't really understand why. If I act obnoxious, is it because I'm an only child? Maybe I'm just obnoxious. If a siblinged person acts obnoxious, maybe it's because he/she has siblings. Perhaps that obnoxious middle child would have turned out to be the Dalai Frickin' Lama if he/she was an only. Ever think of that?

When I ask people about their choice to have a second child, almost all of them say, "We just don't want to have an only child." Why? I can't help but be slightly offended by this. People who seem already overwhelmed by their first baby are having another in order to ensure that they won't have this freak-of-nature only child. I know that this fear doesn't last, and often the second child is loved even more than the first, but still, I think I'm onto something. Is it that everyone is so obsessed with the love and excitement of the first baby that they are dying for another? Is it the same feeling you have after you get your first tattoo and then can't wait to get more ink? Doubtful.

I understand that I will never know the closeness of siblings and sharing family commitments, dramas, responsibilities, but still, I think I am right that most second children are initially desired as a companion for the first and as backup for the future care of the aging parent(s). And yes, they can play with each other. I hear that a lot: "I wanted little Magenta to have someone to play with." Uh . . . what about getting friends? Do you have such little faith that number one will be able to make a friend on its own that you must provide one vaginally? I don't remember ever being bored. I didn't need constant entertainment. In fact, to this day I am pretty OK being on my own (solitary international vacations aside). My parents used to let me bring a friend or cousin on family vacations so I would have a playmate and they could have sex or whatever, but I was happy doing my own thing. I guess I am just wondering why the fear of just one? Does it seem sad or lonely? Are people afraid of being alone themselves, so they are projecting? Are they afraid that the first kid will be a stinker, so they want a backup? I am not a professional family-dynamicologist, but I think I make a decent argument for taking a chill pill, literally. Maybe go back on birth control until you really think this through.

There is one downside that I will take time to mention here because I (clearly) have spent a lot of time thinking about this. Aging/sick parents. I have been lucky so far, and my parents are still married and in general good health. So I don't really worry about them being lonely or ailing, yet. Financially, they have told me not to worry, that they saved money for their golden years, but still, that can be a real burden on someone, financially, emotionally, and time-wise. To not have anyone to help, share the stress, share the cost of medical care, to have to go through all that alone does scare me. Again, I am lucky that my parents have taken care to ensure that I won't be too financially burdened by their needs as they get older, but eventually I will be all alone with the memories of them and what our life was like as I was growing up. It feels a little depressing as I write it, but I have thought a lot about this, and again, there is no guarantee that if I had a brother or sister, he/she would be any help or comfort anyway. How many times do you hear people complain about their siblings and how little they help or how overbearing and controlling they are? I guess the point is you just never know what you're going to get, but I don't think an only child is the worst possible scenario out there.

Now, you might have already guessed, since I've been thinking so much about this, that the topic I'm grappling with right now is whether or not to make one baby of my own. Especially as I transition in my career from best friend to wife/mom I can't help but wonder if I should make that transition in real life as well. Is Hollywood trying to tell me something? My life is complicated. I have a husband. I have two older stepkids, two dogs, and a time-consuming career. I feel stretched so thin sometimes I don't know if there's time and space for a baby. But then what about not having one? Is it worth it to not have one just because I am so busy right now and pulled in so many directions? And is time a reason to have or not have a baby? Shouldn't I be dying for one? I am not. I thought I would be married younger. I thought I would have kids when I was younger. I didn't know I would be a late bloomer in every aspect of my life. Maybe if my stepkids were younger when I met my husband, they would have fulfilled my maternal instincts, but they were pretty much cooked when I came on the scene—though I like that they could potentially be scapegoats for my inability to make this most gigantic decision. I don't know what to do, and I am waiting for a sign, since everyone and their baby tells me I will know when I'm ready. But I know there won't be one, and I have to put on my big-girl pants (or take them off . . .) and make a decision. My husband has recently offered me two additional dogs if I don't have a baby of my own, and I have to say I am seriously considering his offer, although I wouldn't need two, one would be enough.

Dear Diary

I WROTE FORTY-TWO DIARIES TOTAL IF YOU ADD UP everything in the box my mom sent me from her basement and in my bookshelves in my current home. And, after reading most of them, I learned a few things about me, past and present. Past: I loved Jeff Hunt, like, a lot. I loved shopping. I loved cleaning out and reorganizing my possessions. I loved starting over and had great faith that things would be different starting Monday/first day of school/first day of school after holiday vacation/once my closet was cleaned out. Present: Everything I just wrote about the past is still true if I replace the word "school" with anything else. Minus Jeff Hunt.

I have never been so disappointed in myself and my lack of growth as a person as I have been rereading my old journals. I had this (stupid) idea to go through them for this book, that I would find little gems in them, or some inspiration at least, so I could talk about my early years using my own words from those actual earlier years. At first I was excited to find all the old lists I used to make, to read my old thoughts, and to remember what my life was like and who I used to be. I had planned on using them for material. Maybe even copying them down word for word, thinking that they would be funny or charming, that they would provide some insight into what kind of person I had become. I guess that's the reason one keeps a journal, isn't it? To keep tabs on what was happening and to monitor self-development, keep track of memories? But mine have provided nothing short of utter disappointment. As I started to really read them, I realized that I haven't changed at all from 1986 until about three years ago. That means that for twenty-four years I have been the exact same person, making all the same mistakes and all the same promises to myself. There was almost no growth, no change, no movement of any kind in a positive direction in any way. The only thing somewhat comforting is that I think I started out pretty mature for my age. The bad part is that I totally stopped maturing as a person at around thirteen. It's depressing me. I don't know how to handle this discovery. It's kind of sent me into a tailspin. I like thinking of how far I've come as an adult. I like feeling so superior to the old me. I want to think that I am a really evolved person and that all the experiences I've had have propelled me toward the person I am now. I mean, I own a house and have a retirement account! That's, like, really mature, right? But as I read and reread these old journals of mine, I realized that I had hardly evolved at all until I met Dean Johnsen.

Now, I love my husband, he is the greatest person out there, as far as I'm concerned, but I am totally humiliated that I am one of those girls who needed the right man to straighten her out. And by the way, it's not like Dean Johnsen did anything specific or intentional to get me to shape up. Perhaps it's just a coincidence. But as I read my old journal entries, I am appalled at my lack of growth. They start out with me, as a kid, making lists of what I bought when I went shopping with my mom, what boy I had a crush on, and who my current best friend was. As I got a little older, there were lists of what I bought when I went shopping with my friends, what boy I had a crush on, and who my best friend was. Once I left home for college, the entries turned into rants about boys. I devoted entire books to different boyfriends. Just going over and over my relationships, how I was going to be better, love more, stop him from treating me poorly, that I wasn't going to take it anymore, yet, I noticed, never do I write about ending these dramatic relationships, just changing them and myself. There will be two pages about how much I love a particular fellow, then three about how awful he is to me. It's ridiculous. *I* was ridiculous. I can't help but think, why didn't I read these sooner? What if I would have read them immediately after writing them? Would I have realized how stupid I sounded? God, my friends must have hated listening to me.

When I was younger, before I was boyfriend crazy, there were endless entries about who my best friend was and why. In addition to list making, ranking was clearly really important to me, knowing who was who and where they fit into my life. But the worst part of these entries is that I don't even remember some of the names! I called my mom to help me remember, but she didn't either. There is an actual blank in my mind, no face to name, it's freaky. Tracey Vitkay, if you're out there, do you remember me at all? Apparently, you and I were on-again/off-again best friends in the mid- to late 1980s. Do you remember why we couldn't keep it together? According to my diary, you really kept me on my toes, but I don't know what happened to us. Perhaps if I had gotten Facebook, you would have reached out. Maybe not—maybe the past was too painful for you too.

When reading through these diary entries, I seemed obsessed, at a very young age, with finding some contentment with who I was as a person. This is why I think I was into ranking and categorizing everything all the time. I wanted to always know where things stood. What my passions were, what I was devoted to, and how I was devoting myself to these passions. It seems that if everything was in its place, I would find that contentment I craved, yet I never, ever wrote about why I wasn't content. On February 3, 1988, I wrote:

Dear Diary,
  I'm real happy, and finally at ease with myself, I've been looking for this kind of peace for a long time.

I was twelve.

When I was out of college and living in L.A., in addition to the pages and pages devoted to whatever failing relationship I was committed to, I started to add notes from therapy. Yep, I did the L.A. thing and got a shrink, because I was determined to quit making such horrible mistakes, and if I didn't develop new patterns on my own, I was going to spend money I didn't have finding out why I was making these terrible decisions in the first place. When I look back, it seems so easy now. I could have saved myself thousands of dollars, hundreds of hours, and so many tears . . . if I would have just broken up with guys sooner. Here's a tip I have gleaned from the past: if you're not married and you're writing about him in a blank notebook and spending money talking about him with an accredited psychologist, you should probably just break up with him. Seriously. It's only going to get harder as time goes on, so save yourself the money and the time. Get a trainer instead and dump him. God, if I had followed that advice, I'd have the most rockin' body right now. I know I'm simplifying things a bit, but I bet, for most cases, I am right. How long would you spend trying to fit a puzzle piece into a puzzle where it didn't fit? More than a minute? Why do we spend years and hundreds of dollars on therapy and last-ditch-effort vacations trying to make relationships work out that just aren't ever going to? At least I did. Hopefully, you are smarter than me.

  Another obsession that seems to be a running theme throughout these entries and my life thus far is my addiction to simplification. I'm always striving to make my life simpler, yet I consistently add complications to it. I bought a book on how to simplify one's life when I was in high school, and I have entire notebooks devoted to different ways I am going to get it down, once and for all—that once I do this closet clean out, things will change, life will be different, I will finally be a better person. Yet, in my journals, I never seem satisfied. There is a billboard I pass every day here in L.A. that says, "Be happy with nothing and you will be happy with everything." It bummed me out because I realized that I have always been so preoccupied with changing things in order to enjoy my life that I never just enjoyed it. Maybe the real secret to simplifying is to stop buying shit. I should paint a billboard for my driveway that says, "Don't bring home any more crap." There, simplification complete.

So I have forty-two stupid books filled with my discontent and three years of extreme happiness with no record of it at all (OK, there's a lot of Instagrams and a wedding album I will hopefully have paid for and own by the time this book gets released). But some comfort I can find in it all is that I was always trying and willing to be the best me possible, that I wasn't lazy and I didn't give up on people easily, even when I probably should have. And Jeff Hunt, if you're out there, thank you for not ever getting a restraining order, though I wouldn't blame you if you had.

The Manifesto

PEOPLE TALK A LOT ABOUT GOALS. HAVING GOALS for the day, week, month, year. Five-year goals, ten-year goals. You get it. I have always been a very goal-oriented person, not because I like them, but because I learned a long time ago I need deadlines. I need to have dates by which I have to accomplish things. I need structure. So I have a particularly difficult time with the life I've chosen. I hate not having a job—not awesome for an actor. I hate the constant changes that come with my lifestyle—especially not awesome for an actor with stepchildren and two permanent residences.

I've heard nine-to-five jobs called the daily grind. But parts of it seem nice, to know how much money you will make all the time. To be able to take time off to see your friends and family get married or buried. The work clothes have really tempted me—cute skirt suits and mixing up pants and blazers. Unless I have an audition to be a lawyer or business lady, I have no need for a suit in my life. I have an almost unhealthy addiction to *The Mary Tyler Moore Show*, her work looks were just the best, and I can lose myself in the spreads in fashion magazines that detail how to go from work-appropriate to going-out-sexy by just changing from sensible pumps to sexy stilettos, adding a red lip, and switching out your briefcase for a disco bag! *Et voilà*, you're ready to go from cubicle to cocktails. Happy hour is another mystifying fantasy of mine. Not to say that I don't go to happy hour, because, like, duh, four-dollar drinks and three-dollar apps? Yeah, I hit up a happy hour, but my reasons for doing it are financial, not because I just got off work and wanna get a few cheap well drinks with the cute guy from HR.

I know I sound complainy, I know the grass is always . . . yeah yeah yeah. But I have my fantasies: I fantasize about performance reviews and office Christmas parties. Company softball games and calling in sick. Well, this is why I think I became obsessed with to-do lists and having specific goals. I was trying to get some more structure in my days off. I failed. I tried again. I failed again. Then I got (stole) the idea of writing a manifesto. A type of mission statement. I keep trying to pretend that I have a normal life, but I don't. Like, at all. My life is confusing and crazy and busy and then boring, crickets. It's all over the place. It's hard to accomplish daily tasks when I get a call from my manager saying that I have to be on a plane tomorrow at 6:00 a.m. to go to Oakland for a meeting. I have bought countless plane tickets that don't get used. Hotel rooms booked that get canceled. Wedding gifts getting sent because I couldn't deliver them myself. *A lot* of canceling, days before the event. So, I have somewhat given up on having a to-do list, and that does not make me feel like a productive member of society. It makes me feel like a sloth.

But then, years ago, Isabella Rossellini, an Italian treasure, came out with a makeup line called Manifesto. When you bought something from the line (or maybe it was a promo freebie), they gave you a little empty notebook on which to write your own manifesto. I wasn't totally sure what a manifesto was, even though I knew what I thought the word meant. But I figured if I was going to try to write one, I at least owed it to myself to actually look up the meaning. After all, I went to acting school, so a good, traditional college education I did not get (another goal of mine was to educate myself, and *Vogue* does not count). Here is the *Merriam-Webster's* definition of manifesto:

> a written statement declaring publicly the intentions, motives, or views of its issuer.

This word excited me! It is so much more inspiring than a goal. It's like a goal, but in a better outfit. A manifesto is a mission statement. I want to be on a mission! Isn't that so much better than having a lame to-do list? I think a manifesto should sum up how you want to treat your days, what your priorities are, how you deal with people, how you deal with the earth, and how you want to spend your time. It should be a document that teaches you how to slow down and when to speed up. It should inspire you when you read it. And you should read it often. I also feel that manifestos are allowed to change, to evolve. My life plan in my twenties was so different from my life plan for my thirties. Everyone makes New Year's resolutions that last, how long? Really? But this is like a lifelong evolving resolution.

So I challenged myself to write a manifesto. To think about what's important to me. Think about who I love. About what I love. What and who makes me laugh. When do I feel best about myself, and put all that into writing. How do I plan on leaving the planet? Do I care about the planet? What do I care about? If all of my things got taken away, what would still be meaningful to me, besides getting new things? So here is the latest version of my letter to myself.

> Keep your life simple and stylish and earnest.
> Do good and donate your time and money to something
>   you care about.
> Make people laugh.

Be frank.

Always give people a second chance—but rarely a third.

Live light, travel light, and be light.

Forget shit and move on.

Make everyone you love feel loved.

Waste not, want not. Reuse stuff.

Stop trying to get a tan and straighten your hair—you're
    just not made that way.

Go to the movies, go to the library, go to the park.

Try to make every day feel as close to a vacation as
    possible.

Floss.

I forget this stuff a lot, one thing is stolen from a Yogi tea bag, one I found on Pinterest, but if I did a fraction of this, half of the time, I'd think I was a real champion. But I'm a work in progress. I'll probably never be on a company softball team, I have no cubicle in which to store my glittered evening bag, and my days are, if I'm not working, unstructured and disorganized. I have not mastered the art of time management, but I try not to beat myself up about it. There's a lot of peaks and valleys in the life I've chosen, but my mission statement reminds me to focus on what matters most. When life is awesome, it keeps my head from getting too big, and when things are shitty, it reminds me that my life is still pretty awesome.

Meet the Men
Behind *Archer*

DECEMBER 2014

PERHAPS MY FAVORITE JOB EVER IS DOING A VOICE on an animated TV show on FX called *Archer*. It takes only twenty minutes every few weeks to record my role, but it is one of the most rewarding things I do.

But first, let me catch you up on what I've been doing since I finished writing this book. In my personal life I: took a trip to China. Sent my stepdaughter off to college. Watched some friends get married. Watched other friends get divorced. Threw a few fortieth birthday parties (not my own—yet). Buckley almost died. The miracle vet saved his life—again. And I took my stepkids on their first international vacation—it was only to Vancouver, but still, it counts.

As for my career, I've been busy! I worked on five movies, starred in a TV show, shot an ad campaign for Sprint (unless you *literally* never turn on your television, you have seen me in one of these commercials), finished a sixth season of my web series *Reluctantly Healthy*, and recorded another season of *Archer*.

On *Archer* I play Cheryl, the assistant to the CEO of our spy agency, Malory Archer. Cheryl is a billionairess who enjoys asphyxiaphilia and owns an ocelot named Babou. When I first got the script six years ago, I thought it was smart, funny, and naughty—so naughty, in fact, that I thought it would never actually end up on TV. But I underestimated FX. And the fans. After our first season, we went to San Diego Comic-Con and five hundred people showed up to our screening and Q&A. The next year, there were fifteen hundred people. We needed a bigger ballroom. And it's just kind of been like that ever since.

The team behind *Archer* is based in Atlanta, but we voices live all over. We can usually record wherever we are and, within a certain time frame, whenever we're available. We can wear whatever we want, and we don't have to go through hair and make-up. It's the best.

I have really grown to love my *Archer* pals, and they me. They are so smart, funny, thoughtful, and always helpful and supportive. For example, I sent this email to the executive producers—Matt Thompson, Adam Reed, and Casey Willis—a few days ago:

> I am going to write an additional essay for my paperback that comes out in the spring, and I want to talk about *Archer*. Would you/do you have time to help? Maybe we could do a funny email exchange? If not I have two (one) other (slightly less) humorous ideas.
>
> Hearts—
> Judy

Of course Adam Reed wrote back right away!

Fuck off.

This is what I mean! Supportive. And they love when the actors toss ideas to them for upcoming episodes, story arcs, and character development. This was Matt Thompson's response to my request:

> Lately, every time we talk to you about a script, you ask if we could cast Matt Damon in that part. It started off as more serious, with a hunk spy or something, but now it's, "Can the Queen be Matt Damon?"

(Uh, fucking duh. But whatever. I'm never going to stop asking for Matt Damon to be on *Archer*. Unless they threaten to fire me. BUT ONLY THEN.)

Adam adds:

> Asking us to write something funny for you is the equivalent of people asking you to do a funny voicemail greeting for them. Which I bet you're totally snotty about.
>
> Also, what are your two "slightly less humorous" ideas, and how are they less humorous—albeit slightly—than this one? You're better than this. [See? He believes in me!]
>
> I just realized that my little Gmail picture is Burt Reynolds as the Bandit, while Matt's is Dom DeLuise as Captain Chaos from the *Cannonball Run* movies—which not only starred Burt Reynolds but also Sammy Davis, Jr. . . . who is Casey's Gmail picture! Judy, your Gmail picture seems to be of a panda bear suffering from hip dysplasia. Depressing and lame. You should get in on this *Cannonball* action. I was going to say you could be Adrienne Barbeau, but I think you're more of a Tara Buckman. [Sometimes they lose focus, and sometimes when we spend time together I feel slightly left out of their jokes, but I don't mind, because I know deep down in their hearts they care about me.]
>
> Also, I just realized Fred Dryer was in the first *Cannonball*. [PSA for any Fred Dryer fans about to jump on eBay: My copy editor notes that he was actually in the second *Cannonball*.] Matt, we should try to get him on *Archer*. Fuck Matt Damon. Unless Matt

Damon also holds the NFL record for most safeties in a game (two). Which . . . hang on, lemme check Wikipedia . . . no. No, he does not. [I choose to forgive Adam for saying "Fuck Matt Damon." He might just need to rewatch the Bourne movies. People forget.]

We should make somebody at work make a "fuckyeahfred dryer" Tumblr. Wait. Judy, *you* do that. And then we will write your book for you.

CASEY

Are you suggesting a movie adaptation of *Hunter* starring Matt Damon as Rick Hunter and Judy Greer as Dee Dee McCall?

Maybe asking them for help was a bad idea.

ADAM

YESSSSS! YES YES YES YES YES! Only with Fred Dryer instead of Matt Damon. In which case, do we need Judy? Stepfanie Kramer is as gorgeous as ever—plus she can actually sing, if needed, unlike some people. (Named Judy.) Oh. Maybe Judy could play Dee Dee McCall's quirky friend.

Matt Thompson (not Damon) chimes in:

Just getting started, but this is up.
    http://effyeahfreddryer.tumblr.com
    I really want to put Cheryl in a #89 Rams jersey for the next episode. Maybe put a police badge on it.

JUDY

Uh, guys? I don't know who Fred Dryer is. Dean Johnsen (My Husband) says he played for the Rams? He also asked if there might be a part for Merlin Olsen, as long as you're casting ex-Rams.

ADAM

Yeah. Or dead guys. Judy, do you remember Ray Roberts, who was an offensive tackle for the Lions in the '90s? I played high school football with him. One time he told me I should just be myself. Good advice. [Braggart.]

JUDY

I'm starting to remember *Hunter.* So that guy was a Ram? That Tumblr page about Fred Dryer looks like Tim Olyphant. I liked *Scarecrow and Mrs. King.* How did she get that job with Scarecrow? She was just a mom, wasn't she?

ADAM

JUST a mom. Typical.

MATT (NOT DAMON)

Wait. What were the other two ideas?

JUDY

Hold on. I have to take my mom to the airport.

MATT (NOT DAMON)

Ask her what it's like to be just a mom.

JUDY

OK fine! I didn't have any other ideas. I was really counting on you guys. I could describe what kinds of things I wear to a recording session and what state of mind I arrive in. People care about that, I think.

MATT (NOT DAMON)

Unless you arrive in that Ping-Pong-ball suit you wore on *Planet of the Apes,* I do not think anyone cares what you wear to the studio.

ADAM

Not even your mom. I think with a little tweaking this email exchange will push you over the million-units-sold mark.

What about a TV movie? It's called *Hunter: The Torso Murders* and it's about this serial killer who is just leaving women's torsos around Los Angeles. Hunter and Dee Dee McCall come out of retirement to catch the killer. Judy plays one of the torsos' quirky friend.

MATT (NOT DAMON)

And Judy's character (Becky?) gets pissed at the torso because in three days he/she/it was supposed to attend her Ukulele Opera, which Judy asked the torso to write for her.

ADAM

I don't even think this is still Judy's email address.

MATT (NOT DAMON)

Who's Judy?

ADAM

Judy Greer. She played "Quirky Torso" in *Hunter: The Torso Murders.*

MATT (NOT DAMON)

Oh right! Her big catchphrase was, "Say goodbye to these . . . arms and legs."

ADAM

Well played, sir . . . well played.

JUDY

So my catchphrase wouldn't be, "You're not my torso supervisor!"

ADAM

No.

MATT (NOT DAMON)

I'm not sure. Was that one of your catchphrases on *BoJack Horseman?*

Jeez, Matt! Get over it! So I did a one-episode arc on *BoJack Horseman!* BIG DEAL. Maybe I should have emailed *them* for help with this chapter! They would never try to cast me as a torso-only sidekick to two senior TV action stars! This was a total mistake.

Acknowledgments

I am forever in debt to the following people—

Christina Malach. To quote our new favorite server, "You have the shit job. She gets all the fun, she gets all the recognition, she gets all the money." Amazing. I hope this wasn't a shit job for you, but if my first drafts didn't drive you to the bottle, I don't know what would. Thank you. I will never be able to stop thanking you for making my book a book, for making me seem like a writer, and for all the love and consideration you gave to all of my stories and thoughts. I loved this whole process with you. And thank the sweet baby Jesus they don't have WiFi at Zara, or we wouldn't have made one single deadline.

Cait Hoyt. This is all your fault. Thank you for watching all those Reluctantly Healthys and thinking I was funny and had a book in me. I didn't know that about myself, but thank you for seeing it. And thank you for your work on my proposal, I would never have sold it without your notes and editing in the first place. So you see, this really is all your fault. (Hi to Penny!)

All the people I love at Doubleday. Bill Thomas, you said I was a writer. No one ever told me that before. Thank you, it still brings tears to my eyes. Suzanne Herz, Todd Doughty, Joe Gallagher,

John Fontana, Bette Alexander, and Pei Koay, you are my special effects department. Thank you for bringing this book to life.

My amazing team at CAA. Jeremy Plager, thanks for believing in me eleven years ago, believing in me today, and every day in between. Sean Grumman, I love that you never take no for an answer when it comes to my career. Jim Nicolay, when you get me a job, I get to go to work in my pajamas. That might be the best of all . . .

The rest of Team Judy: Fred Toczek, Eric Suddleson, Jillian Fowkes, Annie Schmidt, Tara Friedlander, and Lucille Selig. You guys are so wonderful, hardworking, and so fun to hang out with at all the weird events we have to go to, thank God.

Carter Smith. Thank you forever for shooting my hardcover jacket. Karla Welch, Kemal Harris, Erica Cloud, Traci Franklin, Harry Josh, and Dottie, I will probably never feel more beautiful and glamorous in my life. I cannot thank you enough and I want to take you all to the DMV with me when my driver's license expires, if you're in L.A. and have time? Please?

The geniuses at the Apple Store Genius Bar who were patient and kind to me, didn't laugh at my questions, and kept my computer running while I wrote this book, and especially for bringing it back to life when I killed it and had a nervous breakdown. To my gorgeous (and handsome) contributors: Sarah Dwyer, Kelly McAdams, Sean Gunn, Lola Glaudini, and Janet Higdon. You made me seem way cooler than I am. Except for Janet. You just *had* to tell it like it is, didn't you?

My family, Emilee and Lucas Johnsen, you guys are the best. I didn't even scratch the surface of how awesome it is to be your stepmom. I love you both and am endlessly proud of you. (Still would love it if you ate more greens, but whatever. Someday . . .) Beverly Evans, my other smokin' hot grandma, I am so thankful for all our time together. Judie Johnsen, thanks for raising the greatest man I could ever hope to marry. I am not worthy, but I promise I will continue to try to be.

Thanks to the late Judy Hershman, Frank Evans, and Charles Saucier. I miss them so much every day.

My parents, Mollie and Rich Evans. You guys put up with so much from me, and still do. I cannot believe how much faith you've always had in me. Way more than I have ever or will ever have in myself. You always think I can do it, whatever "it" is. Thank you. And thanks for paying for college. I am just now realizing how much that must have cost.

Dean Johnsen. I wanted to include you in this list, but since you already got single-card billing before the title I'm leaving it to this, I love you.

And . . .

David Gardner. Just in case people don't know, there is no Judy Greer without a David Gardner. So, yeah. He's the boss of me. Thank you, David, for working nonstop and tirelessly for me since the day we met. I can't even imagine what this business would be like without you, but I am sure I wouldn't last a day. Thank you for everything, all the time.